Telling Stories

Telling Stories
A Short Path to Writing Better Software Requirements

Ben Rinzler

Wiley Publishing, Inc.

Telling Stories
Published by
Wiley Publishing, Inc.
10475 Crosspoint Boulevard
Indianapolis, IN 46256
www.wiley.com

Copyright © 2009 by Wiley Publishing, Inc., Indianapolis, Indiana

Published simultaneously in Canada

ISBN: 978-0-470-43700-1

Manufactured in the United States of America

10 9 8 7 6 5 4 3 2 1

Library of Congress Cataloging-in-Publication Data
Rinzler, Ben, 1962-
   Telling stories : a short path to writing better software requirements / Ben Rinzler.
      p. cm.
   Includes index.
   ISBN 978-0-470-43700-1 (pbk.)
   1. Computer software—Development. 2. Technical writing. I. Title.
   QA76.76.D47R57 2009
   005.1—dc22
                                        2008054926

No part of this publication may be reproduced, stored in a retrieval system or transmitted in any form or by any means, electronic, mechanical, photocopying, recording, scanning or otherwise, except as permitted under Sections 107 or 108 of the 1976 United States Copyright Act, without either the prior written permission of the Publisher, or authorization through payment of the appropriate per-copy fee to the Copyright Clearance Center, 222 Rosewood Drive, Danvers, MA 01923, (978) 750-8400, fax (978) 646-8600. Requests to the Publisher for permission should be addressed to the Permissions Department, John Wiley & Sons, Inc., 111 River Street, Hoboken, NJ 07030, (201) 748-6011, fax (201) 748-6008, or online at http://www.wiley.com/go/permissions.

LIMIT OF LIABILITY/DISCLAIMER OF WARRANTY: The publisher and the author make no representations or warranties with respect to the accuracy or completeness of the contents of this work and specifically disclaim all warranties, including without limitation warranties of fitness for a particular purpose. No warranty may be created or extended by sales or promotional materials. The advice and strategies contained herein may not be suitable for every situation. This work is sold with the understanding that the publisher is not engaged in rendering legal, accounting, or other professional services. If professional assistance is required, the services of a competent professional person should be sought. Neither the publisher nor the author shall be liable for damages arising herefrom. The fact that an organization or Web site is referred to in this work as a citation and/or a potential source of further information does not mean that the author or the publisher endorses the information the organization or Web site may provide or recommendations it may make. Further, readers should be aware that Internet Web sites listed in this work may have changed or disappeared between when this work was written and when it is read.

For general information on our other products and services please contact our Customer Care Department within the United States at (877) 762-2974, outside the United States at (317) 572-3993 or fax (317) 572-4002.

TRADEMARKS: Wiley and the Wiley logo are trademarks or registered trademarks of John Wiley & Sons, Inc. and/or its affiliates, in the United States and other countries, and may not be used without written permission. All other trademarks are the property of their respective owners. Wiley Publishing, Inc. is not associated with any product or vendor mentioned in this book.
Wiley also publishes its books in a variety of electronic formats. Some content that appears in print may not be available in electronic books.

The best story I have to tell is how I met my beautiful wife, Beth Ann,
and how she gave me two miraculous children, Lucy and Sam.
This book is wholeheartedly dedicated to them.

About the Author

Ben Rinzler has been both writing about technology and managing writers and analysts for over 20 years. He began his career in technology at firms including Apple and Macromedia (now Adobe) as a technical writer and manager. He later moved to financial services and spent eight years at Morgan Stanley, where he managed a group of over 20 technical writers and business analysts. During this period, he began teaching courses to writers, analysts, developers, and managers in writing software requirements and explaining complex systems. Ben has a history degree from the University of California, Berkeley, and a certification in Analysis and Design of Information Systems from Columbia University. He now works in IT Operational Risk at Mizuho Securities USA. He lives on the Upper West Side of Manhattan with his wife and two children.

Credits

Development Editor
Adaobi Obi Tulton

Production Editor
Liz Britten

Copy Editor
Nancy Rapoport

Editorial Manager
Mary Beth Wakefield

Production Manager
Tim Tate

Vice President and Executive Group Publisher
Richard Swadley

Vice President and Executive Publisher
Barry Pruett

Associate Publisher
Jim Minatel

Project Coordinator, Cover
Lynsey Stanford

Compositor
Maureen Forys,
Happenstance Type-O-Rama

Proofreader
Justin Neely, Word One

Indexer
Jack Lewis

Cover Designer
Michael Trent

Acknowledgments

Many people contributed directly and indirectly to this effort. I am grateful for their thoughtful insights. I would like to personally thank Barbara Giammona, Andrea Herman, James Brown, Rachel Cottone, Nathanael Sandstrom, Kyle Logan, Mathais McKellar, Allison Dorsey, Brian Hackerson, Art Langer, Alan Rinzler, and Jane Melnick.

Contents

Introduction

This book is about writing clear and compelling software requirements documents. It is not a comprehensive guide to managing requirements through the entire software development process. I focus narrowly on writing the requirements document because I believe this vital step has not been well explained. Aside from writing the document, I describe a few basic approaches to planning the requirements process and building the team you'll need to succeed, and I suggest a few strategies for working with the team as you go along. Many excellent books go into these topics in more detail. I will refer to them as I go along.

Many books help you build important skills for the requirements management process. Most are written by analysts, developers, project managers, and consultants, not writers. These books have a bias toward robust requirements processes for large projects executed by full-time analysts. In establishing credibility for these processes and the requirements-analyst profession, the authors sometimes make writing requirements seem very scientific and complex. Some authors are quite successful in describing how to discover and analyze requirements in great detail for engineering purposes. But these engineer-focused processes are often so specialized that nontechnical readers cannot follow them or understand the results. Often the outputs are a multimedia hodge-podge of storyboards, diagrams, spreadsheets, and presentations that are not clear to anyone who did not create them. This book aims to satisfy a need for a brief, clear explanation of an old-fashioned, document-based approach to requirements that works for most purposes.

This book will appeal to a wide range of stakeholders in the requirements process, especially those who are not full-time requirements analysts. I wrote this book with everyone I've known to struggle with the requirements process in mind, including development managers, engineers, project managers, program managers, IT business analysts, business-side analysts, product managers, business users, and technical writers.

The book stands on its own, for now. There are additional graphical examples on the book's Web site at www.wiley.com/go/tellingstories. As the subject continues to evolve, or as readers demand, I may add additional material and templates to the site.

The methods I recommend are refinements, integrations, and a few additions to well-known and proven techniques of documenting requirements. I hope to add value in describing them quickly and showing how to put together the results in an engaging, logical, and readable sequence: a story.

Telling Stories

Telling Stories

1

Intent on a great project to renew the earth, God calls upon Noah, the one man he can trust to carry out his plans. He starts by clearly explaining the problem at hand:

> And God said unto Noah, The end of all flesh is come before me; for the earth is filled with violence through them; and, behold, I will destroy them with the earth.[1]

A forceful and concise communicator, God then details what he wants done in the first phase of the project:

> Make thee an ark of gopher wood; rooms shalt thou make in the ark, and shalt pitch it within and without with pitch.
>
> And this is the fashion which thou shalt make it of: The length of the ark shall be three hundred cubits, the breadth of it fifty cubits, and the height of it thirty cubits.
>
> A window shalt thou make to the ark, and in a cubit shalt thou finish it above; and the door of the ark shalt thou set in the side thereof; with lower, second, and third stories shalt thou make it.

Having explained the basic requirements of the ark, God moves on to the main processes of phase two of the project, beginning with his own action items:

> And, behold, I, even I, do bring a flood of waters upon the earth, to destroy all flesh, wherein is the breath of life, from under heaven; and every thing that is in the earth shall die.

---

[1] Genesis 6:13 (King James).

He then returns to what he requires of Noah:

> But with thee will I establish my covenant; and thou shalt come into the ark, thou, and thy sons, and thy wife, and thy sons' wives with thee.
>
> And of every living thing of all flesh, two of every sort shalt thou bring into the ark, to keep them alive with thee; they shall be male and female.
>
> Of fowls after their kind, and of cattle after their kind, of every creeping thing of the earth after his kind, two of every sort shall come unto thee, to keep them alive.

And mindful of the details, God makes sure Noah brings food sufficient to keep everyone fed through phase three:

> And take thou unto thee of all food that is eaten, and thou shalt gather it to thee; and it shall be for food for thee, and for them.

God doesn't just say, "Go and build an ark." He goes into a lot of detail about what he wants Noah to do. He also explains what is going to happen and why each thing is required, and he associates what is required of Noah with specific events in a logical order. We start with the general project goals, and then we learn about the ark; he warns of the flood, specifies the passenger list and boarding process, and finally, covers the food requirements.

Because God crafts a compelling narrative, Noah clearly understands what he is supposed to do and why, and the project is a success: " ... all that God commanded him, so did he." We, too, still remember the details of Noah's requirements because they are part of a great story.

Of course God has a few advantages in the requirements process that the rest of us do not. We have to work a bit harder and go into more detail, and therein lies the main purpose of this book.

What Must *We* Do?

When you or I need someone to get something at the store, we write a shopping list. When we need a colleague to create a report on quarterly sales, we send an e-mail explaining the exact time period and figures we want. The shopping list and e-mail are simple *requirements documents*. You create a requirements document to explain what you need to someone capable of meeting the need.

If you're clear and precise, you'll probably get what you want. If there is any problem when the thing is done, you have a record of what you asked for and a credible basis for requesting corrections or improvements.

When you want something complicated, you must write a more detailed requirements document. And when you're explaining not only your own needs, but also the needs of a group, you must find a way to include the group of needers in your process and systematically find out what they want. (God didn't have this issue. He knew what he wanted in an ark and didn't have to reach consensus.) Once you've written something, you have to check back with the needers to make sure you are correctly expressing their needs. If the needers can't make sense of what you've written, they can't tell you if you got it right.

Just as God does with Noah, we do better if we explain what we want in plain language and a clear and logical sequence. We do better when we tell a story.

This book explains how to write a software requirements document using storytelling, the most ancient and human means for sharing information. I know you can't make a software requirements document into a story as exciting as Noah's Ark or *Huckleberry Finn*. But you can make a narrative that is engaging and easy to follow for the people who have an interest in solving the problem at hand. In the narrative, the problem should be clearly stated at the beginning, and all points should lead to the solution, with each point following from one to the next in a logical sequence of dependent outcomes. It also helps if you use a lot of pictures.

When you need something pretty ordinary that people have been making for a long time, like a chair or a hamburger, you don't usually have to explain what you want in much detail. There are perhaps a few variables you need to specify (with cheese, no fries, medium rare). It's more challenging when you need something complicated and specialized such as a new software system.

Only very skilled and specialized engineers make software, and they have gone to special schools to learn new languages and tools (Java, C#, and so on). These engineers mostly communicate with each other about what they make, using all the special words from these new languages, and pretty soon ordinary people can't understand them very well.

The challenge when trying to write a story about what you want software to do is to make it understandable to two groups that communicate in very different ways: the needers of the software and engineers who make it. If both groups do not understand and approve of your story, it will fail.

Why Do We Learn Better From Stories?

I wouldn't need to explain this to Aesop, the mythical author of *Aesop's Fables*. When he wanted to encourage savings, he didn't lecture on the dangers of poverty, he made up the story of the ant and the grasshopper. There are stories to everything, and our brains are built to listen to them.

Listening to a story makes us experience everything we hear as if we were part of the action. We relate to each event and fill in any details that might be left out. We are able to evaluate and remember each piece of information because it is part of a logical and realistic whole that we validate against our own experience. We compare the story to what we know and if it is believable and the information is important to us, we find it compelling in a way that a simple recitation of the same information could never be.

Admittedly, the story of making or changing most software systems is not that interesting, but if you do your best to relate what the system does to an understandable narrative, it will be much more compelling. In particular, if you emphasize the main problem the project aims to solve and carry it through every stage of your work, it can bring life to detailed requirements and make readers pay attention to information that might otherwise be tedious.

How Do Story Elements Relate to Requirements?

You may remember from your English classes (if you took any) that a story has setting, conflict, characters, plot, point of view, and theme. Let's go through these and explore how each is analogous to a part of the requirements process:

- **Conflict:** The basic problem that you are hoping to solve is the central conflict to resolve in the requirements process. We don't often think of a lack of technology as a conflict, but it is a conflict between an old way of working and a new and better way in the future (we hope).
- **Theme:** The theme is the central concept underlying the solution in your document. Viewed another way, a theme can be a very big requirement, such as the general need for an automated way of validating data in your system.
- **Setting:** A setting is the place and time of the story. In a requirements document, it is important to explain the broader context of the problem you are trying to solve. This could include some general information

about your technology environment, business, industry, economic conditions, or any other general background information that might be useful. You probably don't need a lot about the setting in a requirements document, but a paragraph or two in the executive summary can be very helpful.

- **Plot:** The series of processes that occur in the current and future system are the plot of your requirements document. Like the plot in a story, the events happen in a certain order and the outcome of each affects the later ones. They are what make you eagerly turn pages.
- **Characters:** There are many types of characters in a requirements document: some are people, some are machines or programs. Any entity capable of action can be a character in a requirements document.
- **Point of view:** It can be very useful to take different points of view as you describe different processes, or the same process. Your ultimate goal is to provide an omniscient view that faithfully describes everything that happens and what everyone needs. But along the way, it could make sense to explain an order process from *both* the customer and the order-taker point of view, for example.

If we learn best from stories, and if story elements are analogous to elements of a software requirements document, how do we put this idea into practice and make a better requirements document? First, I have to clarify what I mean by *software requirements document*.

What Are *Software* Requirements, and Who Are They For?

A software requirements document explains a business problem and the requirements of a software solution from a user *and* a business perspective. It is precise and detailed so that engineers can figure out what to build and how to evaluate what they produce. It uses common language that the business users and managers on the project can understand. You won't know if the requirements are right unless the needers tell you so, and they can't tell you if they can't understand the document.

Here are some qualities of effective requirements:

- A requirements document states *what* is needed from a system in precise, measurable, and testable terms.

- A requirements document details the way a system interacts with the elements around it.
- A requirements document uses plain language understandable to software users and engineers alike.

There are some very common wrong ideas and misconceptions about requirements documents:

- A requirements document does not explain *how* a system is built.
- A requirements document does not describe the technology used to make a system.
- A requirements document does not detail the schedule, plans, costs, or resources required to make the system.

Beyond its immediate utility to the needers of the software and the engineers making it, a requirements document has many secondary purposes:

- It sells a project to senior management and other stakeholders.
- It demonstrates that a thorough and well-considered process has taken place.
- It preserves a team's reasoning so that future team members can understand how choices were made.
- It provides the basis for functional specifications and acceptance tests.
- It can be a starting point for user documentation.

Are Software Requirements Different from Business Requirements?

Not in this book. I use the term *software requirements* very broadly to mean any requirements for making or changing software systems. Most of what I cover applies to any type of requirements, but some analysts attach a great deal of meaning to the term *software* in the phrase *software requirements*. Sometimes you will hear a great effort made to distinguish software requirements from business requirements, technical requirements, functional requirements, nonfunctional requirements, minimum daily requirements, and so on.

Having tangled with several of these terms in various environments and projects, I can confidently tell you there is no clear consensus about what they mean and how they should be used. When engaged to work on any type of requirements, you should not assume you know what to do just because someone told you to go write "business" requirements, "software" requirements, or any other type.

I have often heard "business" requirements defined as requirements written by a nontechnical "business-side" group and then delivered to a "technical" group that analyzes them and then devises "software" requirements that are more technical and detailed. But I have also heard "business" requirements used to describe all types of nontechnical requirements.

I don't think dividing requirements into many categories is a very useful exercise. Using the approach I recommend, distinctions aren't really important. When gathering requirements, it can help to think of meaningful categories that remind people of what they might have overlooked. These categories are usually more specific than abstract terms such as "software" and "business." Think about performance requirements, data requirements, usability requirements, availability requirements, or any other category that is meaningful to your project. I'll make more specific suggestions when I discuss gathering content. I think it's best to focus on telling the main story of the system; every type of requirement will come up along the way.

Why Projects Collapse
(Without Detailed Requirements)

To understand how a project can break down without effective written requirements, let's take a look at a fictional, but very typical story.

When starting a project to make a new order processing system, the makers and needers of the software have a few meetings. The makers listen to the basic ideas of what the needers want and very quickly get into talking among themselves about how they are going to build something to satisfy the needers. The needers can't follow the discussion, but try to participate by smiling and nodding.

After retreating to their offices, the makers present the needers with something in writing about what they are going to do and ask the needers to approve it. They call it a requirements document, but it says more about *how* the makers are going to do their work than the details of *what* they are making. There are considerable details about costs and resources and schedules, but nothing clear about things such as how to apply the discount rate for preferred customers and whether a customer profile can be altered from the transaction entry screen by users without customer service entitlements.

The needers, who don't want to seem stupid or mean in challenging the knowledge of the makers, haplessly approve the "requirements" document and go about their business. Who has time to read a document like this? The first 50 pages are lists of data fields and data types followed by a printout of a PowerPoint presentation with bullet points that say "State of the Art," "Secure Solution," and "Peak Performance." It's hard to know what these mean, but they sound impressive.

Besides, the needers don't feel like they should have to do a lot of work at this point, because after all, they are paying someone to meet *their* needs; let the makers figure it out. And what they need is so obvious. Anyone with a decent background in accounting knows the basics of transaction processing and can adapt it to this line of business. The manager of the makers seems so clever and smiles nicely as if she understands exactly what to do.

The makers disappear for three weeks and come back with a prototype of what they call the *interface* to show the needers. None of the needers dare to ask what an interface is. The makers show the needers several pictures of screens and the needers get some idea of how they will use the new system. Someone asks how they can apply a discount rate for preferred customers and the makers say that will be added later. No one takes notes. There are several more meetings showing different versions. The same person asks about the discount rate again and the makers show them where the discount field is on the customer-profile screen. The needers are reasonably happy with what they see (when they're paying attention), even if it is missing some details. The system goes into production. Soon, a customer calls up angry because he was not given his usual discount.

It turns out that no one who enters transactions has access to the customer-profile screen where it's possible to add the discount rate, and it would raise regulatory issues about segregation of duties if they did. Without substantially changing the architecture of the whole system, the only way to apply the discount is with a post-sale credit that takes a full day at the end of the month for a staff member to manually calculate with spreadsheets. Not an optimal outcome.

Because the needers and makers did not understand each other well enough and didn't spend enough time on requirements, the system doesn't meet some fundamental needs.

What I just described happened last year. This year, senior management wants to clean up the mess and try to make the system that was supposed to fix everything actually work, so they've drafted you, the hapless project manager, to be the point person to deal with IT. One of the senior managers thinks it would be a good idea to write what she calls a "business requirements document." Or perhaps IT has appointed you, the harried software development manager, to write what they call a "software requirements document."

Why Have We Turned from the Path of Righteousness?

So if writing a requirements document is such an obvious and important thing to do, and the consequences of not doing it are so severe, why is it often not done, or done very badly? This topic leads to an early digression. Knowing the answer to this question is not critical to learning how to write better requirements documents, but I have so often had to defend and justify the very necessity of the effort that I'm certain many of you will, too. It's helpful to understand how things got to be the way they are now and also to be ready to answer common protests about the process.

Let's begin with a brief history of writing software requirements. In the middle of the twentieth century, in the early days of the computer age, it was very expensive and time consuming to develop software. There weren't many engineers and there were few tools to automate their work. The wisest of the mid-century software makers, probably after some missteps, realized the need for writing clear and precise requirements before doing much development work. One of the best, Tom DeMarco, wrote a book named *Structured Analysis and System Specification*[2] that elegantly defined a standard for explaining software systems and writing requirements that came to be known simply as Structured Analysis. Structured Analysis explains systems as a series of processes that are represented in "Data Flow Diagrams." Mini-specs written in "Structured English" explain all of the process, and the "Data Dictionary" and "Data Structure Diagrams" describe and represent all of the system's data. There is more to it, of course, but these are the most important and basic elements. Structured Analysis was the primary way to do this work for most of the twentieth century, and in many ways it still is, especially in large organizations like corporations, government, and the military. Most of the ideas in this book are in some way part of Structured Analysis. The standard I recommend for data flow diagrams comes directly from Structured Analysis and is often called the *Yourdon DeMarco* data flow diagram. (Tom Demarco often partnered with Edward Yourdon, another giant in systems analysis.) An example follows.

---

[2] DeMarco, Tom. *Structured Analysis and System Specification*. Yourdon Press Series

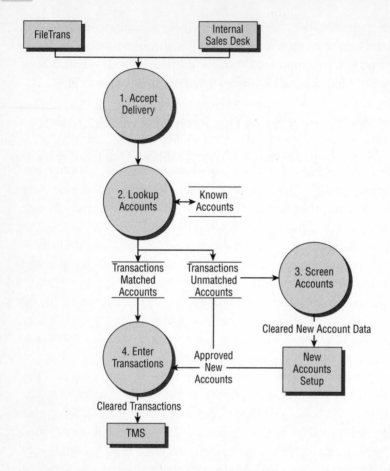

When personal computers hit the mainstream, many more people became programmers and began writing software for all kinds of new purposes. New technologies, programming languages, and authoring tools made writing software much faster and easier. Analysis and documentation, however, were still slow and painful. New technologies and development methodologies challenged some of the basic tenets of Structured Analysis. If you could create working software in less time than it takes to write documentation, why bother? Just get something working as fast as possible and let your users actually use it instead of trying to decipher some long, tedious document. Small groups of engineers worked in garages and produced hugely successful software products. Developers sat next to their customers on trading floors and made changes in seconds. There was no time for requirements analysis on these scrappy teams. Developers often made software a bit at a time, releasing new versions with just a few new features every few months or days.

Now, as the pace of software development continues to speed up, the rigors of Structured Analysis are often considered too time-consuming. Various ways of developing software have evolved to keep up with how software is really being developed. These include Rapid Development, Agile, Extreme Programming, and others. To be fair, most credible developers recommend these less-structured methodologies only when developers can work very closely with their users and freely collaborate. Unfortunately, many projects throw out Structured Analysis (and all analysis, really) without meeting these conditions.

Most new methodologies include good-faith efforts to gather and document requirements. They describe various kinds of meetings or workshops that produce nonnarrative artifacts representing requirements: charts, diagrams, even Post-its. These artifacts are all perfectly clear to everyone in the room during the requirements meeting (except the guy who went to get snacks at a crucial moment). The downfall of these "documentation-lite" approaches is that they assume everyone can understand the artifacts produced by the minimal requirements-writing process and also that the consequences of building something that doesn't meet requirements can be easily rectified. If you weren't in the room when the consensus was reached (and perhaps even if you were) you may not have the exact same understanding of what is to be done as everyone else, and the artifacts may not communicate with enough precision to resolve the ambiguity. Three years later when everyone who worked on the last version has left the company (except the guy who went to get snacks during the requirements meeting), there is no intelligible record of what happened.

As software development becomes a global, commoditized process, requirements documents are again becoming more critical. In today's scattered work place, teams are often separated by oceans. As outsourcing becomes the norm, engineers are unhappily far away from their users and the close collaboration upon which many modern methodologies depend is often not possible. Increasingly, people who need software have to write requirements documents and send them to far-off engineering groups.

The speed of analysis has not kept up with the speed of development, and while programmers have been trained in legions around the world, we have not developed an equivalent population with the skills required to analyze and write requirements. Today we have an enormous need for this work, and few people who can do it. Often the job is imposed on development managers and project managers who lack training in analysis and communication. They often produce far more than is necessary, agonizing for months, producing phone-book-length documents and wall-sized diagrams, and then wondering why their requirements aren't met.

Not surprisingly, many become disillusioned with the requirements process. I don't believe this is because writing requirements is an inherently flawed exercise. I think that the wrong people have been forced to do the work, they haven't been adequately trained or supported, and they usually waste a lot of effort working on the wrong content. People hate writing requirements when they do too much work and produce complex and confusing material.

A simple and flexible storytelling process can be satisfying and adaptable to a wide range of small and large efforts. This approach is even compatible with most of the latest methods of software development, including Agile, Extreme, and others.

I'll explain later who I think should be writing requirements. Now I'll get into how telling stories applies directly to the requirements process.

Can Stories Get Us Back on Track?

Perhaps while exploring many useful ways of representing software systems for engineers, Structured Analysis and other modern methods have become too abstract and moved away from how people ordinarily learn and communicate—too far away from storytelling. Storytelling is something everyone understands intuitively, immediately improving the process of gathering information and structuring the requirements document.

When you tell a story, you instinctively transform abstract knowledge into a logical structure. Whether writing or reading a story, you quickly get bored when you get into material that isn't interesting. You also can tell immediately when something sounds wrong, even if you haven't heard the story before. You get this very sophisticated validation process for free, without having to teach anything to anybody. Your mind is so well suited to stories that it almost automatically eliminates superfluous content and keeps you on the right subject. This quality of stories is especially useful when explaining very complex systems.

Let me tell another story to show how this works. When I switched from writing about software that regular people use to do everyday tasks, to writing about a credit risk system at an investment bank, I floundered for several days. The hardest part was that I couldn't see or use the system. All I could do was look at reports it produced and talk to the development manager, and he wasn't much of a talker. The credit risk system was a series of jobs that ran at night, moving huge quantities of data around and then producing a lot data that credit analysts could query the next day. When the development manager would try to explain it to me (there was no real documentation), he would talk in great detail about what all the parts did and show me schema diagrams and other stuff I couldn't make sense of.

Fortunately, I was at the same time taking a class in analyzing information systems at night. I didn't know it, but I was learning Structured Analysis. The teacher never said anything about stories, but one night he said, "Every system is basically the same. It takes data from somewhere, it does something to it, and then it puts it somewhere else." We also learned a simple form of diagram. (See the example of a Yourdon DeMarco data flow diagram earlier in this chapter.) These diagrams showed data moving between what he called "processes." Each process was an action that changed data (not a thing). The lights went on.

The next day I asked my development manager to explain his system in a different way. "Let's say your system is a lumber mill. The data your system works with is like the wood the lumber mill processes. I want you to tell me the story of how your lumber mill makes wood products, starting with the trees in the forest and ending up with finish-grade plywood."

From then on, it was easy. We started with where all the data came from and I made him explain everything that happened to it until all the different kinds of finished data were saved at the end. Along the way he explained what was required at each step. I didn't write very many notes in prose as I had been doing previously, but drew diagrams with descriptive names for processes and data.

Thinking of what I was doing as writing a story made everything fall into place. Even if what I was producing looked pretty "techy," it moved along and made sense the same way a story does.

Making Structured Analysis into a Story

I've made some grandiose claims about the ability of telling stories to rescue the requirements-writing process. I've also discussed Structured Analysis and how it defines the basic tools of analysis that I believe are the best ways to approach requirements writing. Those of you who know something about Structured Analysis may puzzle over how I embrace these two approaches. The results of Structured Analysis are usually not considered a narrative. Many of the strongest proponents of Structured Analysis (including Tom DeMarco himself, writing in *Structured Analysis and System Specification*) touted its advantages over what they called "narrative prose" analysis documents. I don't know exactly what they meant by that, but I can guess that they were criticizing the long, rambling documents I've seen that have a lot of text and no meaningful structure or systematic methodology. *Brain dump* is a more common and perhaps better term for documents like this.

Interestingly, near the end of *Structured Analysis*, DeMarco includes instructions for what he calls "packaging" the results of structured analysis. He doesn't call for any summary or narrative content to tie it all together. He does recommend including a guide to Structured Analysis that explains how all the tools work. He acknowledges that the methods of Structured Analysis will be new to many people. Instead of narrative about the content of the work itself, we get narrative about the tools. I don't think users reviewing requirements really want to know anything about Structured Analysis. This reminds me of those "How to use this book" sections I always find amusing. "Begin with Chapter 1 and turn each page to the left to proceed. Bold type means the content is important!" If a book *needs* a "How to use this book" section to be understood, it has already failed.

There is a middle ground, however, between rambling, unstructured "narrative" and nonnarrative collections of diagrams, specifications, and data dictionaries that only those who know Structured Analysis can understand. My "story" approach takes simplified versions of the most basic Structured Analysis tools and puts them in a narrative structure that explains itself as it goes along. There's no need for a separate "How to read a story" section.

One key advantage of Structured Analysis, according to its authors, was that parts could stand on their own, be distributed for review independently, created out of order, and didn't have to be read as a monolithic phone book.

The parts of a good narrative document can also be created out of order and read on their own. In fact, I recommend starting with data flow diagrams. A bit of narrative content that explains how a diagram fits into the overall system makes it *more* capable of being understood on its own, not less. It's very easy for readers to skim or skip around in a well-structured document in which every section explains how it fits into the whole. One of the biggest problems I've observed when analysts distribute parts of their "nonnarrative" work is they leave off meaningful titles and there is not a brief summary that explains the basic purpose of the current part.

I can't tell you the number of times I've had to strenuously search through carefully crafted, richly detailed diagrams and code descriptions trying to figure out the basic purpose and name of the system under discussion.

My favorite example was a 400-page functional spec for an equity trading system that did not say anywhere in the entire document that the system was for trading equities. I was trying to prove to regulators that the system was documented, and for lack of about six words ("TraderX is for trading equities") the 400 pages were useless as evidence.

Narrative does not have to be rambling, incoherent, and unstructured. It can be as clear and precise as any diagram, table, equation, or code. It just has to be done right. Diagrams, tables, equations, and code can be a lot clearer and more compelling with just a little bit of good old-fashioned narrative support. Disparagers of the power of narrative are usually just bad at it, or they've never been taught.

To win over the nonnarrators, I have to broaden their ideas about narrative. Narrative doesn't have to be long paragraphs, few headings, and no pictures. You can tell a story in pictures, text, video, audio, dance, or any other media, and you can mix and match as you see fit. The key thing is that the media are effective in getting your point across, and that there is logical, meaningful structure to the material in which the parts build on each other from beginning to end.

In creating an effective narrative form for a software requirements document, I use a mix of very specific elements:

- Clear, precise words
- Clear, short sentences
- Clear, short paragraphs
- A strong overall structure that breaks up all the content into short sections with meaningful titles, organized by subject
- Lots of diagrams (data flow diagrams, to be specific) showing every process in the system
- Structured descriptions of each process
- Descriptions of all the important data in the system
- Summary material that ties it all together

The result doesn't look much like what you think of as a story, but if you pick it up and turn to the first page, you'll find an actual beginning that states the problem, proposes a solution, and then compels you to keep reading. You can go page by page, or skip to the part you care about. Wherever you go, you'll be able to clearly observe how the story has continued. You'll know where you are, what subject is being addressed, and how it fits into the whole. You'll also know where to go to find anything else.

The tools comprising Structured Analysis do not produce what people think of as a story, but there is a story underlying nearly every part—it just doesn't look like an old-fashioned one. Add a bit of summary material before your diagrams and put them in order, and you have a graphic story, more like a comic book than a traditional book, but a story nonetheless.

Who Should Do This Work?

Most of the people I've heard strongly criticize writing software requirements are really good at developing software or managing projects and really bad at writing. With better training and support, some people who feel this way can produce adequate requirements, but there is no escaping their fundamental distaste for the work. After much strenuous effort to work around and with those who hate writing requirements, I've come to agree with them. Great software developers and project managers have many wonderful talents, but writing usually isn't one of them.

Why not get people who are really good writers to do it? When you know Beethoven and Shakespeare, you don't force Beethoven to write you a sonnet; you call Shakespeare. Why have we been forcing software developers to do a writer's job? Where are all the requirements writers?

There aren't many working in IT departments, consulting firms, and software companies. These organizations have become so focused on what they consider "technical" skills that you will have a hard time finding anyone who can write in many of them. I became frustrated with the recruiting process at a firm where I used to work when I found that its college recruiting targeted only computer science majors. I asked one of the recruiters what percentage of the IT jobs at the firm were best filled by computer science majors. The answer was maybe 40 percent, definitely less than half. What about all the other jobs? No answer. I have nothing against computer science majors, but when I interviewed them, only a few had any English or even liberal arts classes on their transcripts.

Why isn't writing English considered an important technical skill? Who is going to write the documentation, the proposals, the presentations, the announcements, and the e-mails, let alone the software requirements? There are now far more people who can write good Java code working in technology than can write a clear sentence. When it comes time to write requirements, it honestly doesn't occur to many people working in technology to go find a writer; they've never met one, and there aren't any on staff.

Education has been emphasizing science, math, and engineering for over a generation and writing has been devalued as a professional skill, left to liberal arts majors, poets, novelists, journalists, and other miscreants.

There are, however, a few hardy souls hidden in technology companies and IT departments who can skim this book and report for duty tomorrow, ready to write requirements better than most of the people doing the work now. Strangely, many of these people do not know what software requirements are. They are called *technical writers*. Most often they write end-user documentation: online help systems, manuals, website content, runbooks, and the like. The best are those writing technical documentation for engineers: functional specifications, programming manuals, operations guides, and so on.

Good technical writers usually begin with strong writing skills and have learned enough technology to work well with engineers and developers to communicate effectively with a wide range of end users and technology people. Many have participated in the software development process enough to understand much of the nuance and language. They have worked on many projects and are good at interviewing subject matter experts and learning technology quickly. They can also write a lot faster and better, and therefore cheaper, than software developers or business users. Of course they do not start out with the information in their heads, so it may seem like more time is required for interviews and subsequent reviews. But overall, technical writers require much less of important people's time than developers do in writing requirements. (As a former technical writer, I have to confess a strong bias in discussing our advantages in the requirements process.)

Aside from software development managers and project managers, the most common title for writers of requirements is *business analyst* or *requirements analyst*. These analysts come from a wide variety of backgrounds. Some are former developers who found they liked the work better than programming, some were project managers, and some worked in a line of business and managed the relationship with the software developers. Some of these analysts are excellent at their jobs, but most are better at what they started out doing than they are at writing and communicating.

With better support and training, many of the people pressed into service writing requirements today, regardless of education or background, could do a better job, and many people who aren't doing it at all could be taught.

If you're one of those having this work imposed on you and you really think you're the wrong person for the job, you should have no shame in making it known. Tell your boss the firm could save money and free you up to do what you're good at if it would hire a technical writer to write requirements.

If you can't get a technical writer or a good business analyst, this book should be helpful to you as a starting point. If you don't like to write or think you are bad at writing, I encourage you to write as little as possible. The most text-heavy documents I've seen were written by engineers and included many pages of superfluous material. Follow the guidelines in this book and stick to short, punchy sections, paragraphs, and sentences. Use lots of diagrams and if you see more than an inch or two of text anywhere, break it up. Remember, a comic book is usually a very good story.

Summary

My advice breaks down to just a few essential points. First there are some very general ones, some of which we've gone into already:

- Stories are the best way to communicate requirements.
- We approach writing requirements like you are telling a story.
- Story elements such as conflict, theme, plot, and character are directly analogous to the requirements process.
- Software requirements explain a business problem and the requirements of a software solution in nontechnical language.
- Software requirements do not include project management details such as schedule, resources, and cost.
- There is no well-understood distinction between *software* requirements and *business* requirements.
- Structured Analysis defined the basic tools for specifying requirements in 1979 and has remained an important methodology ever since.
- Structured Analysis did not include a narrative structure to hold all of its parts together.
- Combining the basic elements of Structured Analysis with a simple narrative structure results in a much more effective final document.
- Technical writers are best suited to writing requirements, but others can adequately do the work with some training and practice.

Having discussed these general ideas about requirements and stories, I'll thoroughly describe specific skills and tools, beginning with three skills that may be new to you:

- Write clear and precise words, sentences, and paragraphs that specify testable requirements.
- Create data flow diagrams simple enough for anyone to follow, but sufficiently rigorous and precise to be useful to engineers.
- Explain processes systematically to capture all the vital information and requirements.
- Associate requirements with processes. Write requirements using precise terms and with a measurable outcome.
- Create a system inventory that includes every element of the system: every known process, actor, output, report, category of data, and anything that the team thinks is important about the system.
- Break down the system into a series of events or processes so that they form a linear story of what happens at every step.
- Structure this information in a logical sequence, including an executive summary, the current state, future state, data descriptions, and various summary sections and optional appendixes for handling specialized material specific to certain projects.
- Maintain and reuse requirements content when writing test plans, user documentation, functional specifications, and other materials.

The rest of this book covers this advice in considerably more detail. The next chapter starts where the story begins, with clear and precise words, sentences, and paragraphs.

The Language of Your Story

2

So far I've avoided the most difficult point: how to write. Of course I cannot explain how to write well in this book. I can only describe some qualities of good writing that are especially important to writing requirements and recommend some other resources. I do hope I can at least inspire some hope and make a few simple suggestions.

The language of requirements must be clear and precise to all potential readers. It must define a specific, *measurable* outcome.

How to do this? The answer involves learning a bit about writing. As a rarely taught subject, software writing is overly mystified by those who haven't done it much. It *is* difficult to write beautifully, but it's not that hard to be clear. Writing is more like playing guitar than violin. After only a few lessons, most people can play a few simple songs, have fun, and get a point across playing the guitar. Most beginners sound terrible on the violin for several years.

If you don't try anything too fancy in writing, you can usually get your point across and be clear, even convincing, without being a virtuoso. Most bad writers get into trouble because they try to do too much and quickly strangle the meaning of their work.

Clarity, brevity, and precision are vital qualities of effective requirements writing. Let's consider these concepts.

Clarity

Clarity is not a divine gift that some have and some don't. True, some writers are exceptionally clear and others struggle to be barely comprehensible. But clarity is simple. You can learn how and get better with practice. Clarity requires humility. Rid yourself of any desire to impress your reader with the vastness and complexity of your knowledge. Carefully consider what your readers can understand and make sure to build that understanding slowly and systematically so readers can learn new ideas and accept new information.

Let's start with the two most fundamental parts of writing: words and sentences.

Here's a very simple rule you shouldn't forget:

Use Words Your Reader Understands

That doesn't sound complicated does it? Well, people struggle with it—a lot. In particular, members of big organizations and technologists tend to use a lot of specialized words, jargon, and especially acronyms or abbreviations that are understood only by the small group that uses those words often. These words sometimes save a lot of time, especially acronyms, but writers need to be mindful that specialized words are not understood outside the group.

Controlling privileged information is one of the most basic kinds of power available to us. Using unknown words can make us seem more powerful to people outside of our group. There is a part of us that wants this power and is threatened by clarity. We want to be in the exclusive group that knows the magic words. Learn to recognize and control this part of yourself and you will write more clearly.

In the requirements process, analysts commonly use many unclear words. Sometimes I think technologists don't believe they have a new idea unless they come up with a new and complicated-sounding term for it. Creating acronyms is the worst example of this tendency. Some people seem to deliberately create acronyms to make common terms seem mysterious and powerful. Count the syllables of the original phrase and the abbreviation. If you're not saving more than 10 syllables, don't use the abbreviation. Remember that virtually no one outside of your group can understand a newly made acronym.

Sometimes special terms are so commonly used inside a certain group that group members start using the special terms unconsciously as if they were commonly understood. I discovered a great example of this right at the beginning of the otherwise very clear *Structured Analysis and System Specification*. Tom DeMarco and P.J. Plauger (who wrote the forward) use the acronym EDP without defining what the letters stand for. This term must have been so common among system analysts in 1979 that it didn't occur to either DeMarco or Plauger to stop and define it. If you're a fish writing for other fish, you don't need to define water. But just 30 years later I have to stop and wonder what they mean. I'm guessing electronic data processing from the context. (Plauger praises Tom for his "wealth of EDP experience." Demarco says "…it was easier to train computer people to understand the application than to train users to understand EDP technology.")

Common abbreviations I hear in the requirements world that save hardly any effort and confuse a lot of people are BRD (business requirements document),

DFD (data flow diagram), DD (data dictionary), UAT (user acceptance testing), ERD (entity relationship diagram—okay , that's hard to say—say "schema diagram" instead). Is it really that hard to say three words?

Careful with *It*

So far I've talked about overly specialized and complicated words, but these aren't the only words that confuse people. Pronouns can be really confusing, too. Complicated words are too specialized, and pronouns often aren't specialized enough. Pronouns take the place of nouns when you want to avoid repetition and streamline a sentence. They replace specific nouns such as New Yorkers, Bob, or table, with all-purpose variable nouns such as they, him, or it.

A pronoun can cause confusion because the more words you put between the original specific word you started with, and the all-purpose variable word you replaced it with, the less likely you are to remember what the original "it" was. You get a weird feeling of being lost in the sentence when "it" gets used too often. It's not as if the "it" doesn't mean anything and "it" can't be part of a good sentence. You just kind of lose track of "it," what is being discussed. As you may have now. What is *it*? *It's* what I'm referring to. You're not sure what I mean are you? That's because I have gone on too long without reminding you what *it* is: a pronoun.

A pronoun is a lot like an abbreviation. It's a short, unclear word that replaces a long, clear word so you can communicate faster. Being concise is generally a good thing, but with both acronyms and pronouns, you should frequently remind readers of the longer, clearer words. A pronoun should immediately follow the noun it replaces, and an acronym should be redefined in at least every major section of your document.

Search the Internet for lots of great examples of misused pronouns. Here are a couple of examples similar to what you might encounter writing requirements:

> Account number and validation are vital to completed transactions. They must be carefully reviewed.

Does "they" refer to "account number and validation" or "completed transactions"? What must be carefully reviewed?

> The sales team informs customer service that it is responsible for new accounts.

Um … I thought you were supposed to do it.

Don't Make Up New Terms

In many—really most—cases, you don't need to make up a fancy new title for a new way of doing things. When I'm reading a book like this one and I read something like, "Requirements are best written in Structured English,"[1] I get anxious. Another complicated thing I don't know and have to learn. Instead, why not just describe what you mean without inventing a new term. Instead of using the term "Structured English" in this book, I simply say it's best to write short, clear, and precise sentences that are telling the reader to do something. I explain that if there is a condition, say "If the condition is met, then do this … Otherwise do that …" I don't go into a lot of complicated explanations of how it is like or unlike writing programming code.

Write Short Sentences with a Clear Actor and Action

So if you're using good, clear, and simple words, the next trick is to string them together so they say something. The technical jargon of grammarians is nearly as complicated and obtuse as that of technology people. I found a great explanation of how sentences work in Joe Williams' book *Style: Toward Clarity and Grace*.[2] To summarize, every sentence has an actor and an action. An actor isn't always a person; sometimes it's a thing or an idea, or some other entity capable of doing something. If you read a sentence and you can't figure out who (or what) is the actor and what is the action, the sentence isn't clear.

Most bad writers aren't clear because they write long, complicated sentences that hide the actor and the action. Consider this sentence:

---

[1] Caine, Stephan H., and Kent E. Gordon. "PDL—A Tool For Software Design." National Computer Conference Proceedings, 44: 271–276. (1975).

[2] Joe Williams, *Style: Toward Clarity and Grace*,(Chicago, IL: University of Chicago Press, 1995.)

It is widely understood that among the requisites for better understanding of control deficiencies is a plausible understanding of a complete and executable risk-and-control framework defining, among other things, the fundamental primary areas of logical security control, physical control, change management control, and operational control over all critical aspects of the technology environment.

Well that sounds pretty fancy, but where is the actor? Where is the action? It's hard to tell. Let's think about what the writer really wants to say. Something about what you need to know about a "control framework" before you can understand "control deficiencies." Who is the actor? The writer doesn't say. This sentence is written in what grammarians call the *passive voice* because it doesn't specify who the actor is. This kind of writing is bad for all purposes, but in requirements writing it's plain wrong. When writing requirements, you must specify the actor (the person or thing responsible for doing something).

Let's surmise the actor should be the reader. We could address the reader as "you" (the *second person* in grammar speak). We can also leave out a lot of empty, wordy modifiers and break it up into two sentences:

You understand control deficiencies better if you completely understand the risk-and-control framework. A risk-and-control framework defines logical security controls, physical controls, change management controls, and operational controls in the technology environment.

This is a lot clearer. We can make it stronger still if we skip the niceties and just give orders using the *declarative* or *imperative* tense. Declarative sentences are crisp, sometimes blunt (or rude-sounding). But a declaration is really the clearest and simplest way to put together a requirement, and I strongly recommend using this type of sentence wherever possible in a requirements document. It saves a lot of needless words and awkward constructions. It also sounds a lot more forceful and holds the reader's attention better. Observe how much better our example works as a declarative sentence:

To understand control deficiencies, learn the controls for logical security, physical security, change management, and operations defined in the control framework.

"You" are the clear actor of the sentence, but because I'm addressing you directly, I don't have to write "you." I also took out a lot of needless words, producing a much shorter, stronger, clearer statement.

Clear *and* Concise

Being concise means writing as little as possible. It isn't always clearer to say less. Sometimes it helps to break things down and fully and carefully explain each part. But in general, and this is especially true for less advanced writers, the more you write, the less clear you are. Be especially mindful of wordiness. "Wordiness" means using a lot of words that don't significantly add to or modify the basic meaning. You can remove many of the words in most sentences without losing any meaning. Get in the habit of rereading all your work and eliminating needless words.

Let's give it a try:

You can remove many of the words in most sentences without the sentence losing any meaning.

- Removing words from sentences often doesn't remove meaning.
- Removing words doesn't remove meaning.
- Remove words not meaning.
- Remove extra words.

Maybe the last one is more concise than clear. You get the point. After some practice, you'll find this process easy and fun. When eliminating words, look for the following:

- Irrelevant information
- Unnecessary qualifiers and introductions (My favorite is "In my humble opinion..." Why do you ever need to say that? Readers can make their own decisions about your opinion.)
- Repetitive structures
- Complicated words
- Laborious, lengthy descriptions of the obvious

The following example, modified only slightly from its original (to protect the guilty), includes all of these unfortunate qualities:

> Examiners will need to insert the name of the application used to authorize personnel to implement entitlement changes in the "Authorization Utility" column. Examiners will need to insert what evidence is in place to support the operation of this control in the "Evidence of Control" column. Examiners will need to indicate in the "Adequacy of Control Design" column their assessment of the control (Adequate or Inadequate). In the "Control - App Specific" column, describe the process development managers follow and the evidence retained to periodically review access to turnover systems, production IDs, data and code for their application to ensure that access is limited to only the people that require access as described in the "Observed Control- Standard" column and the Consolidated Regulatory Guidelines Document. At the Authorization Manager's discretion, the Coordinator may be asked to assess and/or update the information requested in preparation for the Certification Manager's review.

Let's get out the machete. First, we can address the reader directly and get rid of all this indirect, repetitive "Examiners will indicate … " verbiage. The verb choice is very strange. Why all the inserting? And instead of "evidence is in place to support the operation of this control," can't we just say "evidence"? Why do we have say that appropriate access is described in two different places? And can't we just leave off the bit about the Coordinator possibly being asked to update information? Why must this be explained? If it happens it happens. Also, the long paragraph is unreadable. Let's break it into steps:

1. Enter the name of the application you use to authorize entitlement changes under "Application Utility" and describe the evidence in "Evidence of Control."
2. Choose "Adequate" or "Inadequate" for "Adequacy of Control Design."
3. Under "Observed Control - App Specific," describe the process and evidence retained for reviewing appropriate access to the application's turnover systems, production IDs, data, and code.

That brought us from 147 words to 61. I don't think we lost anything important, do you? We certainly gained a lot of clarity.

I've touched on some of my pet writing topics, but I strongly recommend further reading and exercises if you want to substantially improve your writing. Read *Style* by Joe Williams, and of course *The Elements of Style* by Strunk and White.[3]

Precision

As a story, a requirements document has a requirement of precision that other stories do not. Other stories can use ambiguity to propel the plot forward and maintain excitement. A requirements document must always clearly and exactly explain all points. Most important, the requirements statements themselves must define a specific and *testable* outcome. This means that when you say that something is required, you must provide a way to measure that the requirement has been met. If you say something has to be faster, you have to say how much faster. If you say you want to process more transactions, you have to say how many.

Requirements lack adequate precision when they are vague, ambiguous, or too general in nature. We are all in the habit of speaking in very general terms. Being very general in communication helps avoid offense. Being specific is much harder and can get you in trouble, so try to avoid it.

Let's look at a few vague, ambiguous, and overly general requirements to see what we can learn. Forgive me if this gets repetitious, but I find lots of examples are helpful.

Vague Requirements

A vague requirement is indefinite or indistinct in nature. It does not include enough information to establish exactly how to meet the requirement. How many times have you read something like this in a document?

> The system shall improve data access for the entire sales staff.

---

[3] William Strunk and E.B. White, *The Elements of Style*, 4th ed. (New York, NY: Longman, 1999).

"Improve" means almost nothing. Does the author mean faster access for those who have it now, access for those who don't have it, or more different types of data? We can't tell. The requirement would be better with more detailed information about who gets access to what data, and for what purpose, like this:

> The system shall provide all operations staff access to all nonarchived transactions for ad hoc querying with the firm's standard query tools.

Let's look at another example:

> The system shall be able to read the new feed from MarcitData.

"Read" and "the new feed" are vague. The author hasn't specified what will be "read" and what happens to the data. We could improve it by describing the data that will be read, what will be done with it, and how fast.

> The system shall be able to import market data for commodity options supplied by MarcitData to the Transaction Management System for pricing of all commodity options transactions with less than 10 seconds latency to the market (see Appendix L for a MarcitData Commodity Options feed specification).

Ambiguous Requirements

An ambiguous requirement can have multiple ("ambi-") meanings. It may sound precise but it defines the desired result in terms that can be interpreted in more than one way. Consider this example:

> The database must present a survey form accessible to all team members showing all current control issues.

"Survey" is ambiguous. It implies that each team member's response is recorded separately for polling purposes. Will the system present the same form to the whole team? Does each team member get their own form? "Database" is unnecessary. We have to resolve this confusion to make the requirements sufficiently precise:

> The system must allow all team members to view and edit the same record of current control issues.

Here is another example of an ambiguous requirement:

> The Reporting function shall provide complete historical reporting capabilities.

We have to define what we mean by "historical reporting capabilities" including both the period and the data available:

> The Reporting function must be able to report on all commodity options transactions for the past three calendar years.

Overly General Requirements

A general requirement pertains to overall qualities and is not specific enough to be helpful:

> The system must improve productivity by 10%.

"Productivity" can mean a lot of things. We have to say exactly what we would like to improve and how:

> The system shall increase the capacity of successful transaction processing by at least 10% each business day.

Here is another overly general requirement:

> The system shall bring about significant cost reductions in transaction processing.

Again, "significant" is too general. What is significant, 5 percent or 50 percent? We need something we can measure:

> The system shall decrease the average cost per transaction by at least 10%.

The Dangers of Technology Words

Technology words are problematic because they sound very specific even when they're not. People who don't understand the technology often misuse the terms.

> Transactions must be accessible through an Application Program Interface (API).

What transactions? API can mean a lot of things. This is both too technical and imprecise. Take out the fancy word and explain what you really need:

> All nonarchived commodity options transactions must be accessible to the firm's standard ad hoc query and reporting tools.

Current, popular buzzwords are especially problematic:

> The system shall enable full virtualization of the trading platform.

I won't even try to explain all the possible meanings of "virtualization." Suffice it to say that it is not a clear and precise word and it has no place in a requirements document. The following is a plausible rewrite:

> The system shall allow traders to run all functions from any desktop system meeting the minimum requirements in the company network.

Imprecise, Buzzword-Laden Management-Speak Summaries

Be clear and precise not only in your detailed requirements statements and other descriptions, but also in your summaries. Summaries can set the tone for a clear and compelling document, or they can incapacitate the reader with meaningless muck.

Politicians and senior managers are masters, of vague buzzwords. In aspiring to senior management, many requirements analysts adopt a similar approach, especially in their executive summaries.

> As we move to bring online next generation technology to optimize our processes, it's vital that we maximize throughput in all our modalities. As part of our suite of efforts to bring this about, the next phase of TransProc will feature real-time, straight-through processing.

This paragraph includes no precise terms. Let's look at all the main words in the paragraph and see what we can do to make them more precise. Because there is so much vague language, I'm going to pretend I did some research so I can supply some missing detail.

Bad	Better
As we bring online next generation technology	As we gather requirements for the next version of TransProc ...
maximize throughput in all our modalities	we must increase transaction processing capacity by 50% at peak trading levels ...
As part of the suite of efforts to bring this about	This will be one part of a larger effort that will also include adding new network capacity and outside transaction sources ...
TransProc will feature real-time, straight-through processing	A transaction will go directly from sales to settlement in less than ten seconds without any manual effort

Even if you do make statements like this reasonably clear and straightforward, you don't need many of them in a requirements document. In Chapter 7, I go into much more detail about summary material in general, and the executive summary in particular.

A Paragraph Is a Short Subject

Paragraphs break up text into small, more-digestible parts, each about a single subject. You should be able to fit at least three paragraphs on a page. Longer paragraphs are intimidating and tend to confuse readers. Make sure all your paragraphs have a clear subject; start a new paragraph when you change subjects. Make sure the first sentence states the subject of the paragraph.

The paragraph that follows is too long. You get tired looking at it. The material is all related to the same subject, but it covers many points and is hard to follow.

> In the current system, electronically delivered transaction files are viewed on paper or on screen and then manually screened and entered into TMS. Roughly 30% of the firm's revenue depends on the timely and accurate processing of these transactions. This process remains from when all transactions were delivered from the sales office on paper, or by telephone. The operations team currently does an admirable job of keeping up with the increasing flow of transactions while maintaining the firm's account screening standards, but there is broad consensus in the project team that the operations group cannot expand its capacity to keep up with the projected business growth. In particular, the account screening process is entirely manual and there is significant risk of overlooking a suspicious new account or failing to notice an illegal trading pattern. The current manual system performs a critical function in validating accounts and enforcing anti-money laundering policies. New staff cannot be trained rapidly enough to bring adequate expertise to the screening process. While screening will always require manual intervention, automating the simple processes will allow staff to focus where their judgment is really required. Additionally, given that the transaction data is already entered in a structured system, it is wasteful and unnecessary to manually reenter it into TMS. Roughly half of new accounts result from electronically delivered transaction files. For external transactions, the system depends on the vendor FileTrans to securely deliver transaction files. Internal files are manually copied to a shared folder.

Notice how much easier it is to read if I just break it into three paragraphs. I have also included the subject of each paragraph:

[*Problems associated with the manual entry process*] In the current system, electronically delivered transaction files are viewed on paper or on screen and then manually screened and entered into TMS. Roughly 30% of the firm's revenue depends on the timely and accurate processing of these transactions. This process remains from when all transactions were delivered from the sales office on paper, or by telephone. The operations team currently does an admirable job of keeping up with the increasing flow of transactions while maintaining the firm's account screening standards, but there is broad consensus in the project team that the operations group cannot expand its capacity to keep up with the projected business growth.

[*Importance of the manual account screening*] The account screening process is entirely manual and there is significant risk of overlooking a suspicious new account or failing to notice an illegal trading pattern. The current system performs a critical function in validating accounts and enforcing anti-money laundering policies. New staff cannot be trained rapidly enough to bring adequate expertise to the screening process. While screening will always require manual intervention, automating the simple processes will allow staff to focus where their judgment is really required.

[*Redundancy of effort*] Additionally, given that the transaction data is already entered in a structured system, it is wasteful and unnecessary to manually reenter it into TMS. Roughly half of new accounts result from electronically delivered transaction files. For external transactions, the system depends on the vendor FileTrans to securely deliver transaction files. Internal files are manually copied to a shared folder.

When you have nothing more to say on a subject, end the paragraph, even if it seems too short. There is nothing wrong with a one-sentence paragraph.

Using a Consistent and Appropriate Level of Detail

"What is the right level of detail?" There is no right answer to this question, but I'm asked it all the time, as if I know. Include as much detail as necessary to achieve the desired outcome. Do not include more detail than will be useful to most of your readers. Once you've decided on a level of detail, stick to it. Don't be very detailed in one part of the document and sketchy in another. I will discuss this issue in greater depth when I get to data flow diagrams and process descriptions.

Summary

This chapter has covered basic language issues as they relate to the requirements process. In particular, this chapter covered the following points:

- Clarity, brevity, and precision are vital to the language of requirements.
- Use commonly understood words. Avoid group-specific terms, technology buzzwords, and acronyms.
- Be careful to properly use pronouns.
- Don't create new terms unless you have to.
- Write short sentences with a clear actor and action.
- Learn to recognize and eliminate vague, ambiguous, and overly general language from requirements and summaries.
- Keep paragraphs short and focused on a single subject.

I've covered many issues about language, but pictures are just as important to the success of a requirements document. Diagrams immediately provide a multidimensional view of a group of processes, showing the big picture of how they fit together in a way that text alone cannot. I devote the entire next chapter to diagrams.

Drawing Pictures

3

Pictures carry much of the story in a good software requirements document. By pictures, I mean diagrams, and not just any diagrams, but a specific type called a *data flow diagram*.

A good data flow diagram can show what a system does, what goes in, what comes out, and where it all goes in much less space and with more precision than is possible with text alone.

A data flow diagram neatly condenses the work of a system into a series of processes and shows the output, products, or data that result from each process. Because of this focus on processes, inputs, and outputs, data flow diagrams are especially well suited to capturing and communicating requirements.

When I teach this, one of my favorite exercises is to choose someone from the class who has no related experience and ask them to tell me what is happening in a diagram like the one that follows.

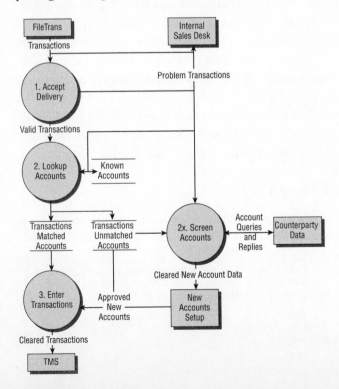

Nearly everyone gets the basic idea and most are able to explain the basic functions of the system in considerable detail.

The data flow diagram exists in various versions. It was formally defined by Larry Constantine in the *IBM Systems Journal* based on Martin and Estrin's "data flow graph" model of computation.[1] Ed Yourdon and Tom Demarco refined and popularized data flow diagramming as a major component of Structured Analysis.[2] Other diagramming techniques have become popular recently among engineers, mainly because they more directly support current software development practices. There is nothing wrong with engineers using these new approaches, but for the less-technical participants in the development process, I have yet to see any diagramming approach communicate better than the classic data flow diagram.

There are different symbol sets commonly used in data flow diagramming. I use the *Yourdon Demarco* symbol set and I've never found a compelling reason to switch. *Gane Sarson* is another effective common standard, but I find it a bit more busy looking. I strongly discourage using complex symbols that have nuanced meanings ("decision points," "recommits," "feedback loops," "interface," and so on). The beauty of this diagramming method is its simplicity. A reader can intuitively grasp the meaning of the diagram without knowing exactly what all the symbols mean.

There are longer, more-formal explanations of data flow diagramming techniques widely available.[3] I am going to focus on what I have found most useful in the field and add some refinements that can help the diagrams to be more clear and readable. As a writer, I also recommend a very strict method for integrating the diagrams with structured text. Many techniques focus on the use of the diagram to capture information. I will focus on the power of the diagram to clearly communicate. The next chapter, "Explaining Processes and Finding Requirements," will describe how to draw the requirements out of these diagrams. For now, I will focus on the basics of data flow diagramming.

Why Data Flow Diagrams?

There are many types of diagrams that might be useful in a requirements document, but the data flow diagram is the most common, critical, and effective.

---

[1] W. Stevens, G. Myers, and L. Constantine, "Structured Design," *IBM Systems Journal*, 13 no. 2 (1974): 115–139. D. Martin and G. Estrin, "Models of Computations and Systems— Evaluation of Vertex Probabilities in Graph Models of Computation," *Journal of the ACM* 14, no. 2 (1967): 281–299.

[2] *Structured Analysis and System Specification*, 1979 Yourdon Press Series by Tom Demarco (Author), P. J. Plauger (Foreword).

[3] One of the best I've seen is Ed Yourdon's explanation on the Structured Analysis wiki site (http://yourdon.com/strucanalysis/wiki/index.php?title=Chapter_9).

Recall that the main purpose of a requirements document is specifying what goes in and what comes out. A requirements document is not about how a system works, what parts it has, or how it is put together. Remember also that the audience of a requirements document is diverse and includes many people from nontechnical backgrounds who may have never read a book about or taken a class in esoteric diagrams.

In a data flow diagram, circles represent stages of work or *processes*, arrows show data moving into or out of processes, parallel lines enclose data stores that show data at rest, and rectangles stand for *externals*, or sources and receivers of data that are not part of the system being documented.

Because a data flow diagram depicts such a simple and abstract level of processes, it can represent nearly any type of activity, not just software systems. Requirements documents are often created as part of a project to automate manual systems. A data flow diagram effectively represents a manual, business, or human process as well as it does a digital process.

Viewed another way, a data flow diagram neatly represents the plot of a story. The major occurrences are processes; the results of the process are data flows that trigger the next action. At each stage there are required actions and results that propel the story forward to its conclusion. Look at the following picture to see how the story of Little Red Riding Hood might look as a data flow diagram.

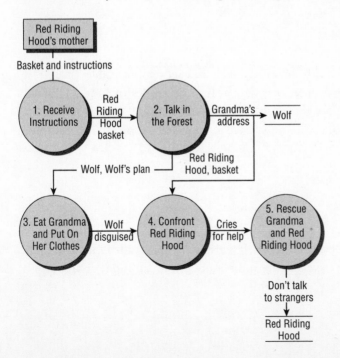

Reading the diagram is very much like reading the story, and although we miss the nuance of the narrative, the diagram does have a certain elegance. We can take in the essence of the story very quickly and completely. Notice that the diagram doesn't show which characters are doing the actions. Also notice that we could have represented the actions in different ways or at different levels of detail. We will explore these issues later in this chapter.

Data Flow Diagram Elements

There are only four components in data flow diagrams: processes, data stores, externals, and data flows. Each element has required parts and can be used only in specific ways.

- **Process:** A process is an action or series of actions that changes data. In the Yourdon Demarco standard, a circle represents a process. Every diagram must have a name that begins with a verb ("Receive Data," "Validate Accounts," "Generate Reports") and a number. Every process must have both an input and an output.

  A process cannot be an entity such as a server, data table, or user.
- **Data store:** A data store is data at rest. Examples include a table in a database, a report, the volatile memory of a computer, or even a person's memory. A data store must have a name and requires either an input or an output.

Known
Accounts

- **Externals:** An external is a source of or destination for data that is not in the scope of the current work. It is also sometimes called a *terminator*. An external must have a name and requires either an input or an output.

- **Data flow:** A data flow represents data moving between processes or to and from externals or data stores. In most cases data flows should be labeled to define exactly what data is moving. When a data flow is connected directly to a well-named data store, the label on the flow may be superfluous. A flow must start from a known point (process, data store, or external) and end at a known point.

- A data flow can split or merge to show how the same kind of data can come from different places and go to the same place, or the opposite.

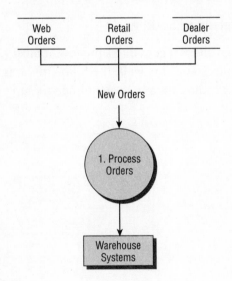

Basic Rules

Every process must have an input and an output. A process must receive data from somewhere and it must send data somewhere. Once you understand that, the other rules follow.

A Process Cannot Create Data

This diagram shows a process spontaneously generating data. Once you've been doing this a while, a construct similar to the following will jump out at you as a mistake.

Data Must Come from an Identified Source

Data cannot appear from nowhere, and if it goes into a process, it must come out in some form. Once you understand this well, the following diagram should look very wrong because its data comes from an unknown source and disappears into the process.

Data Cannot Move or Change by Itself

Data can only be moved or changed by processes. Therefore, data cannot flow directly between data stores or externals, as shown here.

Someone always asks, "If we're only moving data from one place to another, is it really a process?" Yes, a very simple process, but a process nonetheless.

A Diagram Must Begin and End with a Data Store or an External

If a process has to have an input and an output, then a diagram must begin and end with a data store or an external. Otherwise, the data flow would have to begin with a process-generating data or end with a process-destroying data.

Processes Are Actions, Not Entities

A process is a verb, not a noun. If you are having trouble with a diagram and finding a lot of flows going back and forth between the same processes, check to see if any processes are named something like "server," "database," or "customer." These are all entities, not processes, and they will not work properly in a true data flow diagram.

Summary and Detail Diagrams

Data flow diagrams can show systems at any level of detail. Much of the art in creating good diagrams lies in choosing the appropriate levels of detail. In many cases it makes sense to show the big picture and first create diagrams that show an entire system at a summary level, and then create subdiagrams that show greater detail. In summary diagrams, processes may encompass broad areas of work such as "gather data," "screen accounts," or "publish reports." The highest level of diagrams in your document should show how your system fits in with the other systems in your environment. For this reason, these diagrams are sometimes called *context diagrams*. There are formal names for diagrams at other levels of detail, but I prefer not to give you more jargon to remember.

The diagram I showed earlier is an example of a high-level, or summary, diagram.

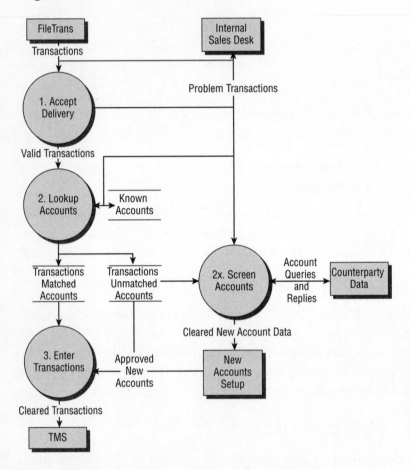

This diagram shows all the work of the system as four simple processes. Notice that there are externals: FileTrans, Internal Sales Desk, Counterparty Data, New Accounts Setup, and TMS. The externals show how the processes of the system fit into the environment in which they function.

It's often very useful to look at a system at this level. Adding requirements to high-level processes can save work. In this example you could specify a series of requirements for the Screen Accounts process that applies to a wide range of subprocesses and different types of data.

When you need to get more detailed, as is usually the case, turn a single process from a summary diagram into another data flow diagram that shows the subprocesses. Sequence all the subprocesses with the number of the summary process and a decimal number. The following diagram is a subdiagram of process 2x, Screen Accounts, in the previous diagram. It shows three subprocesses, numbered 2x.1, 2x.2, and 2x.3. (The "x" is not important to subdiagram numbering. In this case the "x" indicates that Screen Accounts is a process that handles exceptions to normal processing.) Notice also that the subdiagram includes new externals, Internal Counterparty Data and External Counterparty Data. These were represented on the summary diagram just as Counterparty Data. A subdiagram can break down externals and data stores the same way as processes.

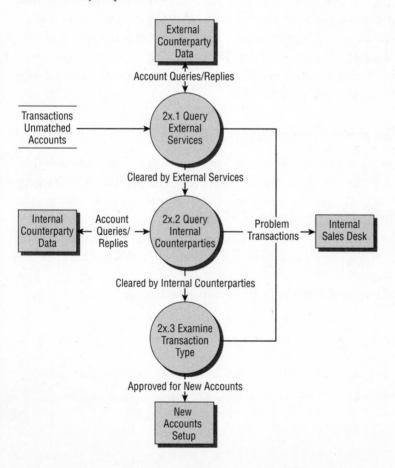

This decimal numbering system for processes makes it very easy to associate a subdiagram with its summary diagram. This is critical in a longer document, which may include hundreds of diagrams.

It's very common to need more detail than what is possible to show in two levels. Use the same system to go down another level and create subprocesses with two decimal places. Process 3.1 could include subprocesses 3.1.1, 3.1.2, 3.1.3, and so on.

Do Not Go More Than Three Levels Deep

More than three levels of hierarchy clutters the organizational structure and reduces the clarity of your document. The numbers also become unreadable and impossible to distinguish. To my eyes 3.1.2.1 is very hard to tell from 3.2.1.2. Technical people seem to love long numbers, but please resist the urge. If you find that your work requires four levels of subdiagrams, you probably made the summary level too abstract. Try promoting some of the processes at the second level to the top level. There's nothing wrong with having a page full of processes at the summary level.

About Creating Rough Diagrams

Most of this chapter is about finishing diagrams so they communicate effectively. While gathering requirements, create rough diagrams and don't worry about the finished product. Focus instead on capturing the basic information and following the basic guidelines of the standard.

I often take very rough notes or, if possible, work quickly in a diagramming application. When I finish an interview, I'm often left with something like the following diagram.

It may take several drafts to make the finished diagram.

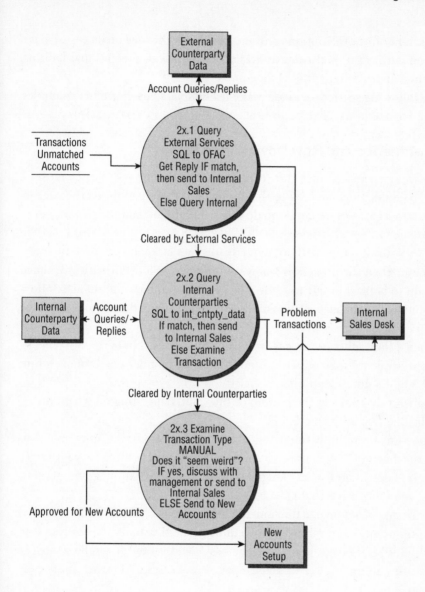

Guidelines for Design Clarity

The basics elements of data flow diagrams are very simple, but it is still quite possible to follow all the rules described so far and create a very confusing diagram. A diagram is a work of visual design and most of us have limited design skills. Fortunately, the data flow diagram standard greatly limits the possible mistakes.

To further limit the options and increase your chances of success, I have come up with additional rules to help you make clear, professional-looking diagrams.

The following sections include many useful examples. For more examples of effective diagrams, check online at www.wiley.com/go/tellingstories.

Start at the Top and Flow Down and to the Left

When we open a book and start reading, where do our eyes go? In most of Western civilization, we look to the top left and then read down the page to the bottom right. We are taught to do this in childhood and the pattern never varies.

Begin your diagram with an external or data store at the top left or top center and align the processes below or to the left in a meaningful sequence from top to bottom or left to right. The process numbers should also follow the direction. Make all (or almost all) of the main data flows move down or to the right.

When a flow splits or merges, you can use various numbering systems to keep the sequence logical. A1, A2, and A3 could number one branch, while B1, B2, and B3 number another.

End your diagrams at the bottom or the right, depending on which direction the diagram is oriented.

(The same ideas apply to readers of right-to-left languages, only opposite. Make the diagram flow in the conventional direction of reading for your target audience. I don't know of any languages read from the bottom up, but if there is one, you know what to do.)

The beauty of automated diagram tools such as Visio is that you freely move processes around and maintain the connections. I usually move processes many times before coming up with the best composition. It can be strangely exhilarating to untangle a jumbled knot of processes and create an elegant diagram.

Align Everything

Misaligned elements make a diagram look cluttered and confusing. Nothing should be placed arbitrarily in your diagrams. The eye must jump around to take in an unaligned group of elements, but it can scan easily across or down a nicely aligned group. Aligned elements are obviously related to each other and the viewer assumes a sequence and a hierarchy from left to right and top to bottom. To make your diagram tell the story of the project very clearly, show the successful outcome as a straight line of processes in your diagram.

Notice in the example diagram I've been using that all the main processes (Accept Delivery, Lookup Accounts, and Enter Transactions) are aligned vertically and numbered in order. The process that results when an account does not match is over on the right, and is numbered differently (2x), to indicate that it is an exception to the successful flow of processes.

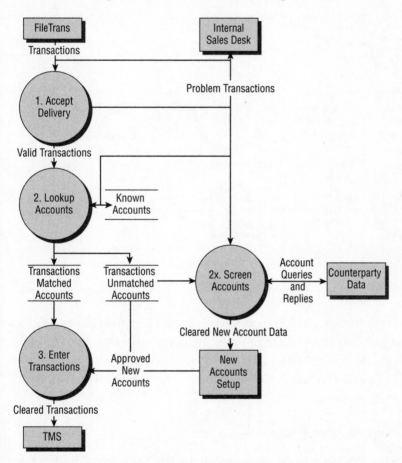

The examples I've used so far have all been well aligned. Notice in the following diagram how misaligning just a few elements makes a diagram look cluttered and confusing.

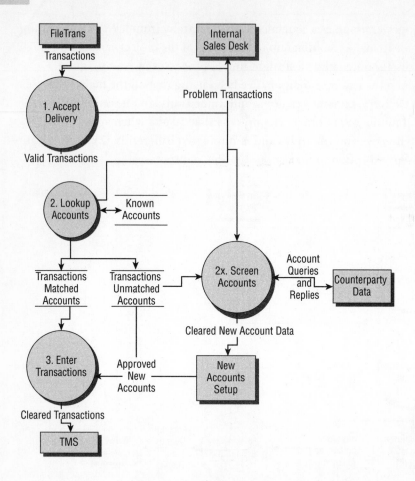

If anything in a diagram is next to something else, it should be aligned vertically to the left edge, center, or right edge of the other object. Likewise, if something is above or below something else, it should be aligned horizontally to the top, center, or bottom of the other object. This is true even for elements that are relatively far apart.

Make Things the Same Size

The more different kinds of things we have to look at, the more we have to take in as we scan a diagram. This makes the brain work harder and causes confusion. When looking at several things that are the exact same size and shape, the brain doesn't have to work as hard looking at each one. It can assume they are part of a meaningful group. For this reason, all your processes should be the same size. In the preceding example, we wonder why Lookup Accounts is smaller in the diagram. Is there something different about it? No, it's just different in the diagram. In most cases, a long name is what forces a process to grow. Consider rewording.

In a big, complex diagram, it can be useful to define two sizes for small and large processes. Make sure the two sizes are very distinct and that there are enough instances of each that they don't look like mistakes. The same goes for data stores and externals, to a lesser degree. I often make them all the same width, but different heights to accommodate more or less text and save space.

Distribute Elements Consistently

It's not enough to align everything; processes, data stores, externals, and any other elements in your diagram should be the same distance apart. If processes are different sizes, or if you are distributing different kinds of elements, try making the centers the same distance apart. Most drawing applications can do this automatically.

Connect at Only Four Points

In nearly every case you should connect to processes, data stores, and externals only at the center of the top, bottom, left, or right edges. If you need to connect more than one flow to the same point, merge the flows prior to connecting, but label them before the merge, as shown in the diagram that follows.

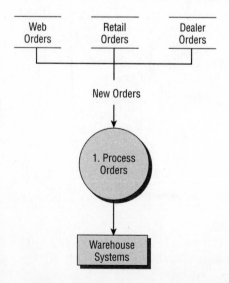

Use Only Straight Lines and 90-Degree Angles

Straight-line data flows are gentler on the eye than curved data flows. A diagram of any size with many curving lines whirling around the processes could be confusing and make your audience dizzy.

Angled lines with different angles also agitate the eye. If you must use angles, use the same angle in every instance, usually a 45-degree angle.

The following diagram shows that even if you follow all the rules for data flow diagramming, bad alignment, curved and angled lines, and out-of-sequence placement of processes can combine to make an overwhelming and confusing diagram. Also note that the diagram is functionally identical to many of the other diagrams in this chapter.

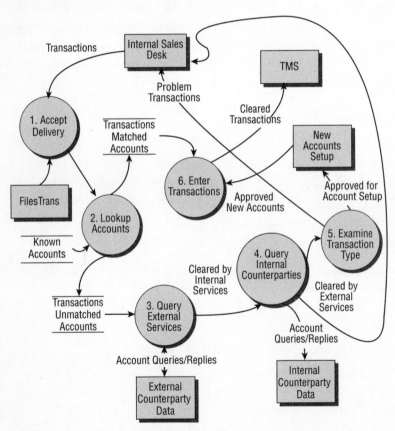

Very talented designers can use curving data flows to beautiful effect, but most of us are not so skilled and are much safer following this rule. If you are trying to achieve a hand-drawn effect, draw the diagram by hand. Trying to replicate hand-drawn lines on a computer usually results in a diagram that look like a mistake.

Consider the Composition and Orientation

Experiment with the overall composition of the diagram. In some cases it makes sense to orient a diagram horizontally so that data flows more left to right than top down. Most of the examples so far have been vertically oriented, but horizontal diagrams can be very useful, especially for online display. You may find some flows work better with a horizontal orientation.

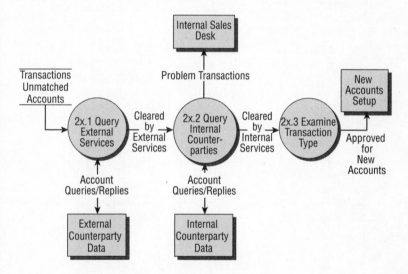

Use the Same Font and Sizes

Use only one font for all the text in your diagram. I prefer a sans serif font such as Arial because it is free of any extra flourishes that can clutter a diagram. If you need to make certain text stand out, use bold or italic styles, or even all caps instead of introducing another font. If you must use a second font, use one for headings and another for the standard text.

Group Related Items and Annotate Diagrams to Add Meaning

If a group of processes or data stores are similar or comprise a meaningful whole, put them near each other and consider drawing a shaded box around them with some kind of identifier like "daily reports," "account validation," or the like.

The rules about assembling data flow diagrams are pretty strict, but there is nothing wrong with adding meaningful annotations outside a diagram. Drawing lightly shaded regions or boxes around portions of diagram can be a good way of showing and naming a group of related processes. Extra text can help streamline process descriptions in a shorter document.

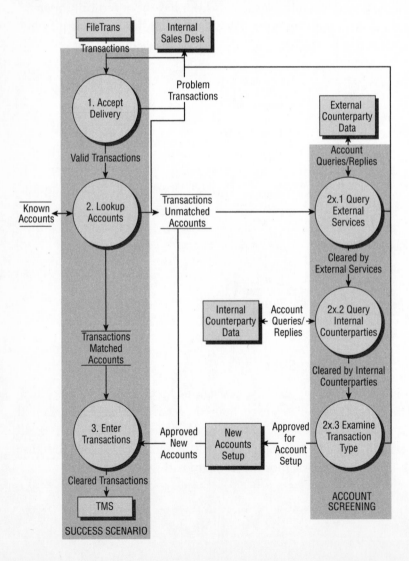

Other Types of Diagrams

Data flow diagrams usually meet all my needs in a requirements document. In fact, if you find yourself needing another type of diagram, it could be a warning sign that your document is going astray and getting into implementation details. That said, it's sometimes necessary to go into a few details about your technical environment, architecture, or other information that isn't well expressed by a data flow diagram.

There are more examples of alternative diagrams at www.wiley.com/go/ tellingstories.

Architecture, Network, and Component Diagrams

This is a loose category of diagrams that show the parts of a whole, or how a bunch of things are connected in a network of some sort. I call them collectively component diagrams because they show the parts of a system instead of showing what the system does. There isn't a strict methodology for creating these diagrams, but all of the design pointers earlier in this chapter are just as meaningful for component diagrams as data flow diagrams.

There is nothing wrong with component diagrams, except when you try to use one to show what a system does instead of just showing all the parts. A component diagram shows nouns; a process flow shows verbs.

The example that follows shows what happens if you try to impose a process flow on a component diagram. Components often do many things, and do them at different stages of different processes. The result is that arrows end up going every which way and it becomes impossible to make sense of the diagram. (This example may seem ridiculous, but I've seen *much* worse.)

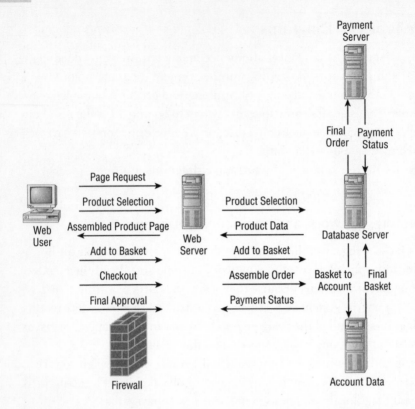

UML Diagrams

The Unified Modeling Language (UML) includes many types of diagrams and is very popular with engineers and system analysts. It is an excellent tool for object-oriented analysis and design. With a few exceptions, I don't find it to be very useful or appropriate for requirements documents.

UML activity diagrams are very similar to the data flow diagrams explained in this chapter. The UML specification for activity diagrams is more complex, especially in the number and meaning of different symbols. (Again, I don't like symbols that require training to understand.) It also lacks some elements, such as process numbers, that would make it easier to combine with text. Its creators, like many engineers, probably don't like to write. If you add process numbers to UML activity diagrams, you can use them effectively in a requirements document (especially if the development team is using UML) but nontechnical readers will definitely be put off. You'll see in the next chapter how process numbers are vital to connecting processes to specific requirements.

Do not use UML use case or class diagrams in a requirements document. They are well suited to engineers in defining all the functionality for objects they are designing and modeling. They are not intended for the general public. Nontechnical people without training in object-oriented design cannot make sense of them. Standard data flow diagrams do a better job of capturing use cases and extracting requirements. After all, a use case is just another series of processes. The following is a simple UML use case diagram.

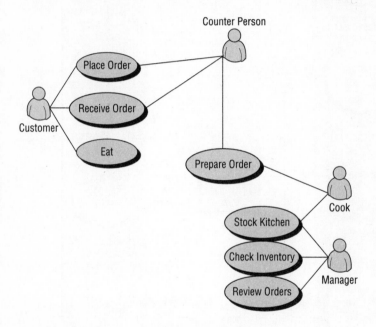

Swim Lanes

Swim lanes are a popular type of diagram that can be adapted to the data flow diagram standard. Swim lanes partition the diagram into horizontal or vertical "lanes" that usually represent the entity that does the work of a process. UML activity diagrams can also be partitioned into swim lanes. If you distribute the processes in the appropriate lanes, you can easily create a diagram that shows who (or what) does what. This approach can make the flow less obvious because arrows must often go back and forth between lanes, but in some cases this is a very effective approach. The example I created earlier to show alignment and annotation could also be a swim lane diagram. I've relabeled the shaded areas to change them into swim lanes showing who does the work of the processes. There are a variety of different formats for swim lanes.

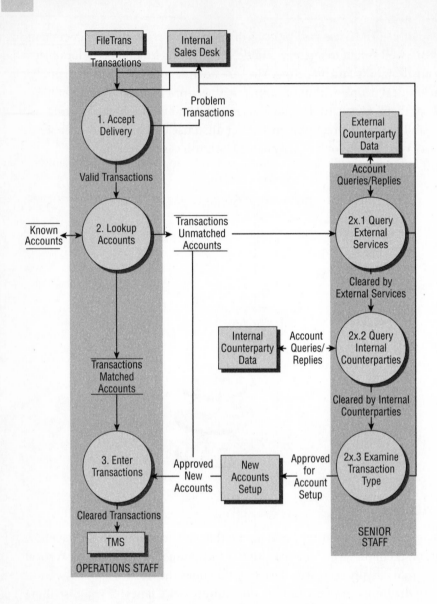

Summary

Data flow diagrams are very good at visually representing workflows, use cases, business processes, or any series of actions.

- Data flow diagrams comprise processes, externals, data stores, and data flows (arrows).

- There are specific rules for using each of these elements: Processes must have an input and an output, and data cannot move unless a process moves it.
- Show different levels of specificity with summary and detail diagrams. A detail diagram shows subprocesses of a single process of the summary, or parent, diagram. Do not go more than three levels deep with detail diagrams.
- Make sure your diagrams show data moving from top to bottom and left to right.
- Use alignment, distribution, straight lines, consistent sizing, and a single font to compose easy-to-read, professional-looking diagrams.
- Avoid other diagram types unless they are really necessary.
- Compose component diagrams following the same guidelines specified for data flow diagrams.
- Avoid UML diagrams, except possibly activity diagrams.
- Arrange data flow diagrams over *swim lanes* when it's very important to show who (or what) is doing the work for every process.
- Use callouts, named regions, and other annotations to add helpful explanations to a data flow diagram.

When I first created a requirements template for developers to use, I included a description field after the data flow diagram and wrote some brief instructions about describing the diagram as necessary and listing requirements. This, unsurprisingly, was a complete failure. I found that people needed a lot more guidance to fully explain everything represented in a diagram.

In the next chapter I will explain how to integrate structured text with data flow diagrams to extract requirements and capture all the important details about processes and data.

Explaining Processes and Finding Requirements

4

Explaining processes in a structured way is a great way of capturing and expressing requirements. A structured explanation forces you to think about what makes a process successful, the precise actions of a process, and what is required for success. Explaining processes works best for discovering functional requirements, but don't limit yourself. Feel free to include any type of requirement that comes up—nonfunctional, organizational, businesses, whatever. There is nothing wrong with capturing redundant requirements, especially in a first draft. You can eliminate duplicates in the review cycle.

Every explanation of a process should include the following:

- **Names and numbers**: The precise name and number of the process being described.
- **Success criteria**: The essential successful result of the process and how exactly to identify and measure it.
- **Started by**: The precondition required to begin the process, usually a triggering event. Depending on the type of process, this can also include the data inputs.
- **Results of**: The end state of the process, including all data outputs, environment changes, and other products of the process that may not be a direct part of the success criteria.
- **Elements of**: The entities involved in the process, including technical components such as servers and software, but also people or groups.
- **Actions in**: The series of events or steps that comprise the successful completion of the process, including exceptions to the successful sequence.
- **Requirements**: The exact functions or conditions that must exist or operate in a certain way in order for the success criteria of the process to be met.

Processes can be high-level or very specific. Adjust the level of detail so that the actions in the process can be described in less than 10 steps. I'm certain that some day we will discover, if we haven't already, that our brains have a difficult time organizing more than 10 things and that it relates directly to how many fingers we have.

You have many choices about how to capture and present this information, but a description that doesn't include most of these elements is incomplete and will likely fail.

Dr. Alistair Cockburn has written well about the need for "casual" and "fully dressed" use cases in his excellent book, *Writing Effective Use Cases*. Because I am not distinguishing between use cases and any other type of process description in this book, I recommend a similar distinction. Again, adjust the scope of your process and the level of detail in each step so that you can describe the action in 3 to 10 steps. It's important to be precise, but too much precision can result in an unreadable, unclear explanation and all of its precise detail will be wasted.

Let's take a more detailed look at each of the elements of process explanations.

Naming Processes

Always put the name and number of the process in the heading at the beginning of the explanation. I don't mean to belabor this very obvious point, but I find that intelligent people often leave out the obvious and thus sabotage their work. I have seen the process name left out many times by very capable people who have put a lot of effort into detailed explanations. Without the name of the process, the detail is disconnected from the whole; all the following information has no relation to the diagram, the system, the scope of work, or anything else. It hangs in space and no one can tell what the author is explaining. Be sure to always use the *exact same* name that appears on the process you are describing in the data flow diagram.

Success Criteria

The success criteria should be included in a brief statement of how the success of the process will be detected, observed, or otherwise measured. Be sure to also consider the fundamental nature of the success to be achieved in the process and how it relates to solving the main problems of the story. You might explain success for a process as something like, "All cleared transactions entered in processing system by 4 p.m. EST." Meeting this condition may actually have almost nothing to do with the real success of the process. A better success criteria statement might be, "The accounts for the buyer and the seller have been identified by the authorized operations clerk as known parties or checked against the most recent available data from the Office of Foreign Assets Control (OFAC). Staff flag cleared transactions and enter them in the transaction processing system."

When describing a high-level process, the success criteria might also include something quite abstract like, "Customer is satisfied with the range and flexibility of our service and continues to do business with us."

Started by

Before a process can begin, a certain state must exist, the expected data must arrive, all the required elements must be in place, and often a specific event has to occur. Describe all of these.

A typical example might be:

- "Customer transaction files are delivered to the transaction file drop-folder by FileTrans."
- "Verification begins at 3 p.m. EST of each business day on which any transactions have occurred."

Results of

In addition to achieving its success criteria (or not), a process also produces other things. Explain everything that the process produces or changes in the environment where it operates. Results are more detailed than success criteria and not always directly related to success. Looking at all the results of a process can also uncover requirements. Do not be overly concerned with results being redundant with success criteria, actions, or requirements. It can be helpful to look at the same information in different ways. Consider the following examples:

- All transactions are marked as Cleared or Not Cleared.
- All cleared transactions are entered in the transaction processing system.
- All customer files are removed from the drop folder and archived.
- Transaction team managers may have received e-mail alerts for escalation of delivery issues.
- Transaction processing is held or resumed based on transaction file delivery status.

Elements of

List *all* the actors of the process. Actors can be any person or thing or system that does something or has something done to it in the course of the process: servers, software, data, Operations Staff Member, accounts receivable, or the User Authentication process.

Actions

The actions drive the process to achieve the success criteria. Describe each step in a declarative sentence using simple words. Write your sentences like this:

> [Actor] [acts] [upon something] [to accomplish something].
>
> Operations Staff Member [actor] reviews [acts] the buyer's account record [upon something] to confirm the account number on the record matches the account number on the order [to accomplish something].

Create a numbered series of actions that describe everything that happens in the process to achieve the success criteria. The great challenge in writing actions is in making a clear story out of what might be a confusing list of random events. Consider the following example:

1. Mother gives Red Riding Hood basket for grandma.
2. Mother instructs Red Riding Hood not to speak to strangers while passing through the forest.
3. Red Riding Hood takes basket and departs.

Exception Handling

Most processes include a variety of possible actions, depending on the results of previous actions. It's very easy to explain a process in which every action has the desired result and proceeds to a single next step, but we all know that there are often many choices to be made at various steps, and often there are unexpected or undesirable results. If we explain everything that could possibly happen at every juncture, we end up with a very confusing explanation and a bad story. Some experts in this field recommend writing a *success scenario* in which every action has the expected result. A success scenario is a very good story, but it has an evil twin: the exception. Success scenarios are often followed by a litany of exceptions, such as this: "Exception to step 5: If the account is invalid, Operations Staff Member calls the buyer and asks him/her to repeat the account number. The process cannot proceed until Operations Staff Member has obtained the correct number. If the buyer's account number is confirmed as being different than the account on the order, Operations Staff Member sends the order to customer service for resolution. See section 782: *Customer Service* for details." Some really important information (that the order can't be processed without a valid account number) is put far away from the action it resulted from. When put after all the other actions, the exception will probably not be read. The put-the-exceptions-after-the-success-scenario approach kills your story.

Try very hard to explain exceptions as you go along, but use formatting and concise language to preserve the clarity and forward momentum of your story. Keep all the really important information together in a logical narrative. Don't make the reader look back and forth to get vital information.

Exception handling is a dangerous trap for the thorough and detail-oriented mind. If you focus too much on exceptions, you are in danger of being *exception driven*. This is a nice piece of jargon that describes the state of paying so much attention to exceptions that you obscure the simple narrative of success.

The opposite problem is not properly focusing on exceptions, or even deliberately ignoring them. The result will be systems that shut down when exceptions occur, or respond in ways that were dreamed up by engineers because nothing was specified in the requirements document.

The right middle path between skimming over exceptions and exhaustively detailing all of the them is, of course, the most difficult to achieve. From my background in technical writing, I've learned a variety of methods to describe branching conditions that are helpful in handling exceptions. All of them combine concise writing with various formatting techniques to distinguish the exception from the flow of the desired actions. I've listed them in the following section according to the magnitude of the possible exceptions.

Indenting Paragraphs That Explain Exceptions

Placing an unnumbered, indented paragraph after a numbered action provides a good place to explain simple exceptions, or anything else you want to add without cluttering the action.

1. Operations Staff Member opens the daily transaction file from the shared folder on the network.

If the file is not there, he calls the FileTrans hotline number and asks a technician the cause of the delay and the estimated time of recovery. If recovery is estimated at two hours or less, he postpones continued processing for the estimated time and then starts the process over again. If longer than two hours, he sends e-mail to the team announcing that because of a FileTrans outage, transactions will not be processed until the next business day.

2.   Operations Staff Member extracts the account numbers from all the transactions in the daily file.

3.   Operations Staff Member compares the transaction account numbers with customers' accounts.

Listing Possible Exceptions as Indented Bullet Points

If a paragraph explaining an exception is getting too long and includes too many branches, it may help to add an indented bulleted list describing each of the possibilities. It's important to put the bullets where the text begins, and not on the left margin where they would interfere with the numbers of the actions. Notice in the following example how, after explaining how to handle several exceptions, I return the reader's focus to the expected actions with a phrase like, "Once he has successfully opened the transaction file … "

1.   Operations Staff Member opens the daily transaction file from the shared folder on the network.

If the file is not there, he calls the FileTrans hotline number and informs a technician that the daily transaction file has not been delivered.

- If recovery is estimated at two hours or less, he postpones continued processing for the estimated time and then starts the process over again.
- If the Operations Staff Member is unable to reach FileTrans after 30 minutes, he e-mails vendor management and requests management escalation.
- If he is unable to reach FileTrans after 30 minutes, he e-mails vendor management and requests management escalation.
- If the delivery estimate is longer than two hours, he sends e-mail to the team announcing that because of a FileTrans outage, transactions will not be processed until the next business day.

2. Once he has successfully opened the transaction file, Operations Staff Member extracts the account numbers from all the transactions in the daily file.

3. Operations Staff Member compares the transaction account numbers with customers' accounts.

Adding an Indented Table with Exceptions and Their Outcomes

If there are more exceptions and possible outcomes than you can handle gracefully in a bulleted list, consider using an indented table. In a table, you can list several possible results in one column and explain the resulting actions in the next. You can even put bullet points or numbered actions inside of a cell in the second column. Although some staunch traditionalists believe that a table is highly disruptive to reading, I think that being able to quickly note several exceptions by scanning down a column without having to read every word lets the reader get back to real reading faster than having to read every word of a long, uninteresting paragraph.

1. Operations Staff Member opens the daily transaction file from the shared folder on the network.

Possible exceptions

If	Then
There is any delay in Operations Staff Member getting the file and beginning processing.	• If the estimated recovery time is before 3:30 EST, Operations Staff Member announces the delay to the Transaction team (verbally or by phone if e-mail is not available), and then starts the process over again at the appointed time. • If the estimated recovery will be after 3:30 EST of the current business day, Operations Staff Member sends an e-mail to the Transaction team announcing that transactions will not be processed until the next business day.

(Continues)

Possible exceptions *(Continued)*

If	Then
An internal system problem prevents Operations Staff Member from getting to the shared folder.	Operations Staff Member calls the help desk and asks for an estimated recovery time.
The file is not in the shared folder.	Operations Staff Member calls FileTrans and reports the problem.
The issue requires FileTrans research.	Operations Staff Member announces a delay to the Transaction team. If FileTrans does not respond in 30 minutes, Operations Staff Member escalates the issue to Transaction team management.
The file is unreadable.	Operations Staff Member calls FileTrans and asks them to regenerate the file.
FileTrans is unreachable for 30 minutes.	Operations Staff Member escalates the issue to Transaction team management.

2. Once he has successfully opened the transaction file, Operations Staff Member extracts the account numbers from all the transactions in the daily file.
3. Operations Staff Member compares the transaction account numbers with customers' accounts.

Notice that the first row in the table defined a response to any kind of delay in processing and the remaining rows explain responses to specific obstacles, all of which involved potential delays. It wasn't necessary to repeat the basic delay response for each exception.

Cross-References to Other Processes

When the complexity of a particular exception is more than you can gracefully handle in a table, make the exception a separate process and use a cross-reference.

> 1. Operations Staff Member opens the daily transaction file from the shared folder on the network.
> 2. Operations Staff Member extracts the account numbers from the transactions in the daily file.
>
>   If the file includes Caymen Mortgage-Backed Credit Derivatives transactions, Operations Staff Member removes those transactions and sends them by e-mail to Mary. See Process 63a, "Process Caymen Mortgage-Backed Credit Derivatives."

With the actions explained, you're ready to state requirements.

Extracting Requirements

Clearly written actions make it easy to find functional requirements. Reread the actions and think about what is required to make each action result in success, and also to handle unsuccessful outcomes.

There is no harm in creating too many requirements in the early drafts of a document. The review process can remove unnecessary or redundant requirements.

As with the actions, use short and simple declarative sentences for requirements statements. Be sure to correctly identify the entity responsible for the requirement and make that entity the subject of the sentence. The requirements statements can be very similar to the actions, but you should think again if they are too similar. Remember that you are capturing only what is required, not everything that is happening. Focus on the outcome.

Language in Requirements

Some analysts use a formal style for requirements statements that nearly always begins with, "The system shall … " While there's nothing technically wrong with it, this approach is wordy and monotonous, and also vague. Avoid repetitive sequences of words and use verbs to state the requirement. No one wants to read a series of sentences, all beginning with, "The system shall … " These are requirements statements; we know they describe what the system shall do. You can leave that out. Alternatively, you can introduce a series of statements with a helpful phrase such as, "The system shall filter data in the following ways … "

Sentences with weak verbs, such as shall, can, or will, that are paired with noun phrases are also inherently more complex and less clear, forceful, and interesting than sentences with strong verb phrases. Compare the following two statements:

> The system shall be able to look at incoming transactions for unknown account numbers.
>
> The system filters unknown account numbers from incoming transactions.

The first few words of the first sentence, "The system shall be able to ... " do not add any meaning or interest.

Numbering Requirements

Number each requirement with the number of the current process. This provides a unique identifier for each requirement and associates it with a specific process. The identifier is a critical tool for tracking the requirement through the development process and prevents confusion. The actual words of the requirement may be too long to conveniently use as an identifier, and they may not be unique.

It's also very helpful to look at a requirement number and know where it came from.

Use the process number and then a decimal point to number requirements. You may also want to add a prefix, such as R for *requirement* or FR for *functional requirement*, so you can tell it from other numbers likely to appear in the document.

The following example shows how some functional requirements might be numbered:

> The system verifies that the account numbers of incoming transactions match account numbers of known and approved customers.
>
> FR 3.1.1: The system alerts Transaction team management by phone and e-mail if the transactions do not arrive by 3:30 EST.
>
> FR 3.1.2: The system immediately informs FileTrans when the transaction file is not present or unreadable and requests correction and recovery time.
>
> FR 3.1.3: The system alerts Transaction team management if FileTrans is unreachable for 30 minutes.

Try to think beyond what is directly executed, especially if you are documenting a process that is already being done, and especially if it's being done manually. Because people know when they've done something, manual processes often don't have signals indicating that certain actions are complete. In our example we may add a requirement that the system indicate that the validation is complete.

> FR 3.1.4: After validating an account, the Operations Staff Member adds a "Validated" or "Not Validated" value to the transaction record.

Some may quibble that a requirement like this is an implementation detail, but requirements about the meaning and content of data are appropriate.

Data Requirements in Process Descriptions

Often while writing functional requirements you will discover data requirements. Data requirements describe new pieces of information that must be captured or changed to achieve the successful outcome of the process. Complete data requirements can be very lengthy and detailed. In general, they don't belong in process descriptions unless you can make them very brief. It is best to state specific requirements about single data fields in a process description and then refer to longer data specifications elsewhere in the document, usually in an appendix.

The example requirement we just created implies that there is a "Validated" field in the transaction record, but we know there isn't one now. We should add something about this:

> DR 3.1.1: The transaction record includes a "Validated" field to record the account validation status of the current transaction. See *Transaction Record Specification* in *Appendix B, Data Specifications*.

I explain more about data specifications in Chapter 5.

Considering Business Rules and Nonfunctional Requirements

Think about any business rules that may be expressed by the actions and make note of them as well. The business rules don't really belong in a process description, but there is no harm mentioning them, or verifying that they are covered elsewhere.

A business rule is implied in our account validation example.

> BZR 3.1: All transactions must be between known entities and accounts that have been screened by OFAC for any record of improper activities.

Make sure that this business rule is listed in the appropriate place in your document.

Process descriptions can also expose nonfunctional requirements, such as proper management support and communication with vendors. In this example, success can depend on a timely response from the vendor, FileTrans, and Transaction team management. Stating these requirements at the process level can highlight the importance of the requirements, but you will probably want to cross-reference a requirement stated elsewhere:

> NFR 3.1: FileTrans must respond within 30 minutes to file delivery queries with a recovery time estimate.
>
> NFR 3.2: Transaction team management must respond to FileTrans issues when FileTrans has not responded or is unreachable for 30 minutes.

Options for Structuring Diagrams and Text

The arrangement of diagrams and text can make a big difference to the success of your document. Choose a structure and a level of detail that work best for all of your audiences, can accommodate the complexity of the project, and can be executed successfully with the time and resources available.

A Formal, Tabular Approach

A tabular approach works well for documents that include a lot of formal detail, particularly when complete coverage of all elements is vital. A table makes it hard to forget parts of an explanation and highlights where descriptions may be thin. This approach takes up more space, but is actually easer to create than more-concise, less-formal structures.

When gathering requirements for any project, I usually put each process description in a table with a row for each part of the description, plus one for notes. In a longer, more-complex document about a big system, it may work best to keep this structure. However, it is not the best format for reading.

Table 4.1 provides an example of a completed process description.

Verify account numbers	
Success Criteria	• The accounts for all the buyers and sellers in all daily transactions have been validated and screened against a database of known suspicious parties.
	• The validated transactions are entered into the transaction settlement system.
Started by	• Customer transaction files are delivered to the transaction file drop folder by FileTrans.
	• Verification begins at 3 p.m. EST of each business day on which any transactions have occurred.
Results of	• All transactions are marked as Cleared or Not Cleared.
	• All cleared transactions are entered in the transaction processing system.
	• All customer files are removed from the drop folder and archived.
	• Transaction team managers may have received e-mail alerts for escalation of delivery issues.
	• Transaction processing is held or resumed based on transaction file delivery status.
Elements of	Customers, shared network infrastructure, operations staff, screening database

(Continues)

Verify account numbers *(Continued)*

Actions

1. FileTrans delivers transaction files to the shared transaction drop folder.

2. Operations Staff Member opens each transaction file from the shared folder on the network.

Possible exceptions

If	Then
There is any delay in Operations Staff Member getting the file and beginning processing	• If the estimated recovery time is before 3:30 p.m. EST, Operations Staff Member announces the delay to the Transaction team (verbally or by phone if e-mail is not available), and then starts the process over again at the appointed time. • If the estimated recovery will be after 3:30 p.m. EST of the current business day, Operations Staff Member sends e-mail to the Transaction team announcing that transactions will not be processed until the next business day.
An internal system problem prevents Operations Staff Member from getting to the shared folder	Operations Staff Member calls the help desk and asks for an estimated recovery time.
The file is not in the shared folder.	Operations Staff Member calls FileTrans and reports the problem.
The issue requires FileTrans research.	Operations Staff Member announces a delay to the transaction team. If File Trans does not respond in 30 minutes, Operations Staff Member escalates the issue to Transaction team management.
FileTrans is unreachable for 30 minutes	Operations Staff Member escalates the issue to Transaction team management.

Verify account numbers *(Continued)*

3. Once he has successfully opened the transaction file, Operations Staff Member extracts the account numbers from all the transactions in the daily file.

4. Operations Staff Member compares the transaction account numbers with known customer accounts.

   - If there are unknown accounts, Operations Staff Member removes them from the transaction file and checks unknown account numbers against the latest Office of Foreign Assets Control (OFAC) database.

   - If there are any matches to suspicious accounts in the OFAC database, the staff member-emails the account number to the Transaction team manager and holds the transaction until the manager responds.

   - For accounts that do not have a match in the OFAC database, the staff member adds the account number to the New Accounts file for processing (see 3.1a, "Add New Accounts").

5. Operations Staff Member enters the validated accounts in the transaction processing system for continued processing.

Requirements

Nonfunctional requirements:

NFR 3.1: FileTrans must respond within 30 minutes to file delivery queries with a recovery time estimate.

NFR 3.2: Transaction team management must respond to FileTrans issues when FileTrans has not responded or is unreachable for 30 minutes.

Business rules:

BZR 3.1: All transactions must be between known entities and accounts that have been screened for any record of improper activities.

Functional requirements:

FR 3.1: FileTrans must deliver all transaction files for daily processing to the transaction file drop folder by 3 p.m. EST.

FR 3.2: Operations Staff alerts Transaction team management by phone and e-mail if the transactions do not arrive by 3:30 EST.

FR 3.3: Operations Staff immediately informs FileTrans when the transaction file is not present or unreadable and requests correction and recovery time.

FR: 3.4: Operations Staff alerts Transaction team management if FileTrans is unreachable for 30 minutes.

(Continues)

Verify account numbers *(Continued)*

Requirements	FR: 3.5: The Account Screening Database is maintained with daily feeds from approved services monitoring suspicious accounts.
	FR 3.6: Accounts for the buyer and seller of each transaction have been identified and cleared for compliance with company transaction guidelines.
	FR. 3.7: Unknown accounts that have no record of suspicious activity are held and researched for new account creation.
Notes	

A Simpler Prose-Based Approach

Old-fashioned prose with a few well-chosen headings can be faster to read and write than a tabular structure, but you must be very confident about including all the required information. This approach is certainly more recognizable when written as a story than when written using the tabular approach. It also requires more writing skills. To save time, we can decide that some possible exceptions are out of scope and leave their resolution to the good sense of others. In our example, we can decide that file delivery issues are not really what the work of the new project is about. We have only two days to come up with some requirements, so we will include only a brief section for Success Criteria, Actions, and Requirements, and we will include only functional requirements. We will identify the actors only as they arise in the actions and we will not detail all the results of the process. Notice how these changes affect the example.

1.1. Verify account numbers

Success Criteria: The account verification process succeeds when the accounts for all the buyers and sellers in daily transactions have been identified and screened against a database of known suspicious parties. The validated transactions are imported to the transaction settlement system.

Actions: Verification begins at 3 p.m. EST each business day on which any transactions have occurred.

1. FileTrans delivers a transaction folder to the shared transaction drop folder.
2. Operations Staff Member opens a daily transaction file from the shared folder on the network.
   If there is a delay in the delivery of the file and estimated recovery time is before 3:30 EST, Operations Staff Member announces the delay to the Transaction team (verbally or by phone if e-mail is not available), and then starts the process over again at the appointed time. If the estimated recovery will be after 3:30 EST, the Operations Staff Member sends an e-mail to the Transaction team announcing that transactions will not be processed until the next business day.
3. Once he has successfully opened the transaction file, Operations Staff Member extracts the account numbers from all the transactions in the daily file.
4. Operations Staff Member compares the transaction account numbers with known customer accounts.
   - If there are unknown accounts, Operations Staff Member removes them from the transaction file and checks unknown account numbers against the Account Screening Database.
   - If there are any matches to suspicious accounts in the database, the staff member e-mails the account number(s) to the transaction(s) team manager and holds the transaction until the manager responds.
   - For accounts that do not have a match in the Account Screening Database, the staff member adds the account number(s) to the New Accounts file for processing (see 3.1a, "Add New Accounts").
5. Operations Staff Member enters the validated accounts in the transaction processing system for continued processing.

Requirements:

FR 3.1: FileTrans must deliver all transaction files for daily processing to the transaction file drop folder by 3 p.m. EST.

FR 3.2: Operations Staff alerts Transaction team management by phone and e-mail if the transactions do not arrive by 3:30 EST.

FR 3.3: Operations Staff alerts Transaction team management if FileTrans is unreachable for 30 minutes.

FR 3.4: The Account Screening Database is maintained with daily feeds from approved services monitoring suspicious accounts.

FR 3.5: Accounts for the buyer and seller of each transaction have been identified and cleared for compliance with company transaction guidelines.

FR. 3.6: Unknown accounts that have no record of suspicious activity are held and researched for new account creation.

An Integrated Diagram and Requirements

If your time is very short and your readers are very impatient with reading documentation, it may be best to put all the information into the diagram itself. You will also have to be comfortable making a lot of assumptions, not detailing some exceptions, and stating only the most basic requirements.

Adding Diagram and Section Introductions

So far, I have covered the information vital to a single process. After you've explained all the processes in a diagram, write an introduction to the diagram that briefly summarizes all of the processes and relates them to the overall story of the document. This small bit of prose is vital narrative glue connecting the parts of your document to form a meaningful story.

While tables and text in diagrams can adequately carry the story of a requirements document through the details of process descriptions and requirements, old-fashioned prose is the best way to write a nice summary introduction.

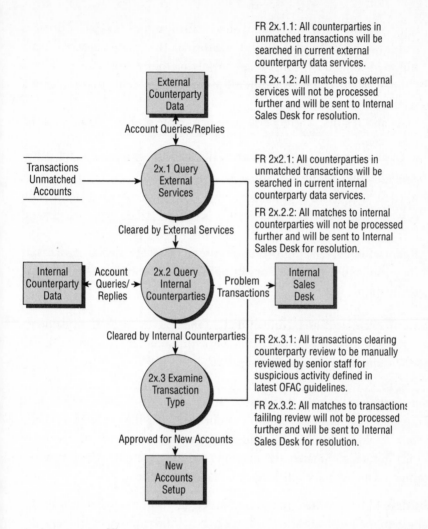

FR 2x.1.1: All counterparties in unmatched transactions will be searched in current external counterparty data services.

FR 2x.1.2: All matches to external services will not be processed further and will be sent to Internal Sales Desk for resolution.

FR 2x2.1: All counterparties in unmatched transactions will be searched in current internal counterparty data services.

FR 2x.2.2: All matches to internal counterparties will not be processed further and will be sent to Internal Sales Desk for resolution.

FR 2x.3.1: All transactions clearing counterparty review to be manually reviewed by senior staff for suspicious activity defined in latest OFAC guidelines.

FR 2x.3.2: All matches to transactions faililng review will not be processed further and will be sent to Internal Sales Desk for resolution.

A summary introduction usually comprises a prose paragraph or two, or possibly a combination of prose and bullet points. It includes most of the same elements as an individual process description. Think of the entire diagram you summarize (or series of diagrams) as a single process and consider including each of the following points, which are very similar to the elements of individual process descriptions. You should not, however, feel obliged to include all of them. Think of the reader skimming the document. The purpose of the summary is to quickly express what is most important and interesting.

- **Name:** A clear name to the overall process or series of processes.

- **Success criteria:** The essential successful result of the entire process and how exactly to identify and measure it. The success described in a summary should explicitly relate to solving the key business problems defined in the overall document, not only the details that indicate a successful outcome.
- **Start and results:** The general state before the process begins, and the end state.
- **Elements:** The entities involved in the process, described much more generally than in the individual process descriptions.
- **Actions:** The series of processes, events, or steps that comprise the successful completion of the overall process, described at a very general level.
- **Requirements:** The high-level requirements of the overall process, if they can be described in a meaningful way—these should not be formally numbered.

Here is an example of an introduction that includes many of these elements in a generalized prose style. Notice that while the summary is high-level, it is very specific about various goals and metrics:

This project must increase the capacity of transaction processing to handle a 40% projected increase in volume without sacrificing the less-than-1% fail rate we have maintained traditionally. We also must maintain our reputation for rigorous automated and manual account screening, which has so far protected us from a single money laundering incident.

In the desired future state, transaction processing will immediately accept orders from the Internal Sales Desk or directly from external customers. If all the accounts match to known counterparties, the order is immediately entered into the Transaction Management System (TMS). If the counterparties aren't known, the system automates the queries of internal and external counterparty data services and then presents cleared transactions for manual approval before passing them to the New Accounts process.

In addition to handling the increased capacity, the new system should be able to enter transactions between known accounts into TMS within 30 minutes.

The account screen of unknown counterparties should not take more than one day.

Summary

You will have to choose the method for explaining processes and the level of detail that work best for your applications, but whatever you choose, you now know what you must include and what you can choose to leave out intentionally. At a minimum, you must do the following:

- Closely tie the explanation of each process to the diagram by using a clear name and number.
- Be sure to specify the elements of the process, the exact success criteria, what starts the process, the basic actions of the process, and the requirements necessary to achieve the success criteria.
- Use indented paragraphs, bulleted lists, or tables to handle exceptions. Don't over-explain exceptions so they obscure the success scenario.
- Number requirements.
- Put data requirements in a separate section, not in the process descriptions (unless they're very short).
- Structure the diagrams and text in a more or less formal way depending on the nature and constraints of the project.
- Write effective summary introductions to diagrams and sections of diagrams that connect the process descriptions to the overall story of the document.

The diagrams described in the previous chapter and the process descriptions explained in this chapter form the bulk of the content in a requirements document. In the next chapter, I explain how to organize this material and structure the entire document.

Finding and Structuring the Content

5

Now that you understand data flow diagrams, process descriptions, and other tools and concepts for crafting the story, it's time to look at how to find the content of your story and structure it in the best way possible.

You will find the content of your story in the minds of the members of the project team. The project team is the group of people assembled by management to plan, manage, and possibly execute the development of the system. You may or may not have any actual authority over the team, but as the person designated to write the requirements document, you must become its voice. Your task is to focus the team on a series of questions that will identify the purpose of the system, its main elements, primary actions, and basic requirements. You must establish a basic rapport with the team and capture information in a way that encourages free communication and respectful listening. You don't have to explain all the theory and methodology behind your process to the team, but you need specific information to get started. Once you have the bulk of this information, you will be ready to write an outline that works for the team and the project.

You Are a Very Important Team Member

Without you, the project team will not be very good at making up its mind and expressing itself with clarity or precision. Members of teams without writers often believe an issue has been resolved to their satisfaction, when in fact different team members may have very different and self-serving notions of the never-written conclusion. As the writer, it is your job to point these out. Often, simply writing down the contradictory conclusion is all that is necessary. As a nonthreatening neutral party, you can clarify differing needs and gently encourage team members to reengage and reach consensus.

The project team produces the content of the requirements document. In writing the requirements document, you hope to capture and express the will of the team. You are not the author of the requirements document; you are the scribe, manager, driver, analyst, and requirements-janitor for the project team. You are not expressing your ideas—you are expressing for the team.

You probably did not choose the team members yourself, but you can possibly have some influence to add members if you think a certain group is not represented. A good project team should have representatives of every major group of stakeholders in the effort. A stakeholder is anyone with something to gain or lose in the deployment of the system. Typically these include, but are not limited to, users (with different functional groupings such as operations, customer service, advisors, and so on), managers, engineers, engineers of dependent systems, engineers of the system your system will depend on, subject matter experts, product managers, marketing people, and support staff.

Building Rapport with the Project Team

Because the project team is the source of nearly all the information that will go in the requirements document, you must find effective ways to get information out of team members. There are many books that provide excellent guidance on how to elicit requirements from project teams, interview subject matter experts, and otherwise troll for requirements. Some include detailed instructions like specialized seating charts, meeting agendas, cookie recipes, trust-building exercises, and the like.

I recommend *Mastering the Requirements Process* by Suzanne and James Robertson (although it doesn't include cookie recipes).

I will mostly focus on the basic information you need to get from the team to get the project started and leave it to your good judgment to find the best ways of getting the information. I will make only a few basic suggestions:

- **Encourage profuse, informal content.** In the initial gathering process, you should encourage team members to freely describe what they do, what the system does, and what the important parts are. The first few meetings or interviews should not be painstakingly detailed. You should focus on quantity more than quality of output. Your later efforts will refine the material you get, and you want to encourage the team members to express themselves freely.
- **Collaborate, repeat, and confirm as you take notes.** As you work, write down what people say in an informal style on a whiteboard, a screen, flip charts, or whatever works best for you. The team must be able to see what you write down and you should ask team members to confirm what you've written using phrases like, "So would it be right to say that the current system effectively identifies invalid accounts?"

- **Meet only when necessary and not for too long.** Don't have too many meetings and don't meet on a regular schedule. A project team meeting should serve a specific purpose; it should not happen because you're supposed to meet every week. Don't meet for longer than two hours: The team may be able to go on longer, but you may not be able to take in what they're saying. Even if you're taping the meeting and taking good notes, you must be able to fully grasp what is being explained. After doing this kind of thing for many years, I've found that the ability to comprehend complex explanations drops off sharply after about 90 minutes. If you're having an all-day series of meetings, be sure to plan several breaks.
- **Meet with individuals or small groups.** Many people are less forthcoming in large group sessions. If you notice someone not participating in a large group, follow up with just that person. For meetings with subject matter experts, you will want to go into considerable detail, which will be tedious for the rest of the group.

Capturing the Critical Information

There is specific information you must capture to begin the project. Pose the following questions to your team to begin the process of getting critical information.

What Are the Business Purposes of the System?

The most important and obvious reasons for doing a project are often not written down because they don't relate directly to functionality. What is obvious and important to the project team may be completely unknown to programmers on the other side of the world. Encourage the team to clearly state what the entire system is supposed to accomplish. These statements will drive many of the functional requirements and business rules. Most important, they will fill in the blanks when other requirements do not cover every possible detail and exception. The more you can do to build greater awareness of the general purpose of the system, the more readers will guess correctly later in the project about how to do something that the team might have overlooked.

These general statements of purpose will also be very important to many summaries, especially the executive summary.

The following are some examples of business reasons:

- Make sure the customer for whom we process transactions has no record or reputation for suspicious activity.
- Make sure that we know and trust the buyer and the seller in every transaction we execute.
- Make sure we can thoroughly research buyers and sellers we don't know as fast as possible, so we can do the right thing and still get the business.
- Make sure we respond to delivery problems fast enough that it's never our fault when there is an overnight transaction delay resulting from a delivery problem.

What Are the Main Elements of the System?

Encourage the team to freely list all the parts of the system to create a comprehensive inventory of the system. This can include any of the actors that play a role in a process: data, hardware, people, teams, or anything important to the system. A system inventory might include items like these:

- Customers
- Operations Staff
- Operations Management
- Customer Transaction Files
- FileTrans
- Shared folder for deliveries
- OFAC database
- Transaction Management System (TMS)
- New accounts report
- Accounts team

What Does the System Do?

Ask the team the basic actions of the system. Don't worry about capturing metrics or using precise language at this stage. Without going into much detail, we'd like to know the system's basic features. These will become the high-level processes you later document in detail. If the team is familiar with the term "use cases" go ahead and ask them for the use cases. Whether you use the term or not, be sure to ask the team to describe what the systems does from the perspective of all types of users and external systems.

A list like this might include the following:

- Matches accounts in transactions to accounts in our customer database
- Checks unknown accounts against the OFAC database
- Handles delivery problems
- Screens account for suspicious activity
- Enters transactions in TMS
- Communicates delivery problems to management
- Sets up new accounts
- Reports suspicious transactions
- Maintains account data

What Is the System Doing Well Now?

You don't want the new system to undo strengths of the current system. Make sure to capture the strong points of the current system. This information will become the starting point of the current state analysis.

- We know it (no training required).
- Transaction processing done by 5 p.m. EST 90% of the time.
- Two operations staff can handle the current transaction volume.
- Transaction fail rate from bad accounts is less that 1%.
- Easy to change process as new screening data become available and laws change.
- Reliable in meeting business objectives: No transactions have been processed with suspicious accounts.

What Is the System Doing Poorly?

Ask the team to name areas where the system does not meet current needs, where it requires too much effort, is too slow, too inflexible, missing vital features, or any other way it disappoints.

You may end up with a list like this one:

- Depends entirely on the knowledge of senior staff
- Can't hire and train staff with sufficient knowledge
- Can't meet expected 50% increase in volume next year
- Although transaction processing is usually done on time, the 10% delay won't be acceptable at higher volumes
- The screening process is entirely manual

What Must the System Continue to Do?

The current system is meeting a variety of requirements already and you must make sure that the new system continues to meet them. The simplest way to gather requirements is just to ask the team what they are. You will get a lengthy list that probably includes the majority of the critical requirements, at least in terms of system outputs. Many requirements you gather in this process may be closely tied to the current system implementation and in reality have no basis in the real business reasons for doing something. For instance you may hear requirements such as, "The LT report has to be submitted to operations by 10 a.m." In a different implementation there may not be a need for that report because all the data is available for querying in real time. Still, at this stage of information gathering just make a note of everything and move on quickly.

The following is an excerpt of a requirements list you might create at this stage of the project. Notice there is no distinction between different types of requirements. At this stage, explaining categories only complicates the process.

- All transactions must be between accounts already in our customer database or accounts that have been screened for any record of improper activities.
- New accounts must be confirmed manually by two staff members in accordance with MegaCorp Account Management Policy and Procedures.
- FileTrans must deliver all transaction files for daily processing to the transaction file drop folder by 3 p.m. EST.
- FileTrans must respond within 30 minutes to file delivery queries with a recovery time estimate.

- Transaction team management must respond to FileTrans issues when FileTrans has not responded or is unreachable for 30 minutes.
- Operations staff alerts Transaction team management if FileTrans is unreachable for 30 minutes.
- The Account Screening Database is maintained with daily feeds from firm-approved services monitoring suspicious accounts.
- Unknown accounts that have no record of suspicious activity are held and researched for new account creation.
- OFAC query for unknown accounts must look for matches by first and last name (including two-character differences), company matches, sovereignty matches, transactional matches, and product matches.

What External Data Does the System Rely On?

Whenever you are changing something, you must keep track of what you cannot change. In systems processing data, you often have little control over the data you must begin with. Ask the team to think of every such instance and keep a list like the following:

- FileTrans file drop
- Format of customer transaction file
- OFAC data structure
- Customer database

What Data Must the System Provide to Other Systems?

Every system must provide data to its users and other systems, often in very specific ways that cannot be changed.

In our example, the system provides data to the following external systems:

- OFAC queries
- Transaction entry in TMS
- New account data
- Delivery alerts

What Do We Hope the New System Will Do Better

Encourage the team to think big and come up with some significant improvements even if they seem unworkable. Ask them to ignore how the system works now and to take a fresh approach to achieving the business purposes they have already described.

Listen respectfully and write down all of the responses. Do not point out why they won't work.

An excerpt of the list might look like this:

- Automate the entire process so no manual effort is required unless a new account has to be created.
- Automatically report delivery problems to FileTrans.
- Get rid of FileTrans.
- Look for long-term patterns of suspicious transactions.
- Process, screen, and enter transactions as soon as they are delivered from customers.
- Prevent delivery of invalid account information requiring validation from customers.

Other Lists

The lists I've mentioned so far are probably necessary for every project, but there are many other things to consider at this stage. These might include security, regulations, more about performance, and so on.

Writing the Outline

After a few meetings with the project team and with key stakeholders, you should have a system inventory that is complete enough for you to write an outline. The outline defines the structure of your document. Your document may have a very different structure depending on the project and the project team, as well as the time and resources available to the project.

What to Include, What to Leave Out

I have to assume that if you are reading this book, you do intend to actually create some sort of requirements documentation. You may face some opposition from the team at this stage and find that you need to advocate for the very existence of a requirements document. Many development methodologies now shamelessly advocate beginning work with little or no requirements documentation.

I have yet to see a project that would not have benefited from at least a small amount of documentation. Every time a group of people comes together and decides what to do, it is good idea to write down what that decision was and check that everyone agrees before anybody does anything. In a long career, I have been repeatedly astounded by the contradictory and self-serving conclusions taken away by different people at the same meeting. Without a precise written record of what was decided, you can never hold anyone accountable for wrongly executing verbal instructions. Developers can choose to skip the functional specification documentation and go straight to writing code, but I have never heard a defensible argument for not capturing at least cursory high-level requirements from the project team.

I have described a robust approach for requirements documentation so far, but I hope you adapt my suggestions to something that is actually possible for your project. If your team uses a rapid or Agile methodology that involves developing working software in small increments with "just enough" documentation, there is no reason why a small increment of documentation cannot be completed along with a small increment of working software. It may be that your team is highly visual and prefers diagrams and screen mock-ups to lengthy runs of prose. There is nothing wrong with more visually oriented documentation. See the diagram in Chapter 4 for an example of visual documentation. The tools I've explained can be adapted to use very little prose.

The small increment of documentation greatly improves the chances that the small amount of working software created will be what the project team intended, and when many of these small documents are completed over time, they can be assembled to make a very useful big document that accurately explains what has transpired.

At the outline stage of the project, you can determine what the team believes is the most concise possible structure of the documentation. For a small, fast-moving project you may choose to document only a single process and its requirements. For a bigger project that requires that you obtain substantial support from other teams and management in a large organization, you may need to create a richly detailed document. At the outline stage, you help the team to decide on the exact contents of the document.

A Generic Outline

In spite of infinite variations, there are elements common to nearly all requirements documents. Few documents include all of these parts, but I will explain them briefly. I explain all of these parts in more detail elsewhere in the book.

- **Executive summary**: A very succinct and forceful summary of the entire document that explains the business problem and the scope of the project, and makes the key recommendations, referring to details elsewhere in the document.
- **Current state**: A high-level summary followed by a series of data flow diagrams and process descriptions explaining how the system functions now while capturing key requirements. For a larger system there may be many subprocesses and summaries of important processes.
- **Future state**: Identical to the current state in structure, but explains how the new or changed system will function.
- **Gap analysis**: An analytical section, usually including tables that highlight the differences between current and future state processes and requirements.
- **Requirements summary**: A series of tables grouping different types of requirements in various ways that are useful for the project.
- **Appendixes**: Reference material that is vital to the document but is not part of the narrative thrust of the main document. Typical appendixes include data descriptions, report descriptions, user interface requirements, security requirements, and so on.

An Agile Outline

If the team wants to use a fast-moving Agile approach, you probably cannot and should not outline the entire work before the developers create working software. Instead, plan on creating small portions as the team works, usually one process at a time.

In our example, an Agile outline might look something like this:

Summary

- Business Purpose
- Success Criteria

Nonfunctional Requirements

- Business Rules

Future State (skip the current state)

Data Requirements

A Robust Outline

In spite of popular rebellions against monolithic requirements documentation, there will probably always be a need for exactly that. Larger organizations benefit from, and often demand, a more complete requirements document before development can begin. When writing a longer outline, it helps to briefly describe the content you intend to put in each section. The outline of a complete requirements document might look something like this:

Executive Summary

- **Problem:** The account delivery screening process is too manual, labor intensive, and inconsistent. It cannot scale to meet projected demand.
- **Recommendation:** Build an automated system while maintaining or exceeding current performance and quality standards.
- **Key requirements and success criteria:** Immediate processing of transactions upon delivery, automated delivery-problem alerts, automated OFAC screening, automated transaction entry for screened transactions.
- **Scope:** No changes to Transaction Management System (TMS), no change to account setup, no changes to OFAC database.

Current State

- Summary
- Transaction file delivery
- Account matching
- OFAC screening of unknown accounts
- Screening for suspicious activity
- Transaction entry
- Reporting suspicious transactions
- New accounts setup
- Account maintenance

Future State

- Summary
- Transaction file delivery
- Account matching and screening
- Transaction entry

Gap Analysis

- Screening standards current (manual) vs. future (automated)
- Transaction entry validation current (manual) vs. future (automated)

Requirements Summary

- Comprehensive summary
- Nonfunctional requirements
- Business rules
- Screening requirements
- Delivery requirements

Appendixes

- Data Descriptions: Transaction data, account data, OFAC data
- Report Descriptions: Delivery alerts, suspicious activity alert, processing status alert
- User Interface Requirements: Interface design committee process, usability testing

Summary

This chapter has explained how to work with the project team to outline the content of the requirements document. The chapter recommended the following:

- Build rapport with the project team. Manage time with the team very carefully, meeting with small groups and individuals.
- Gather critical information to build the system inventory: basic elements, current strengths, and current weaknesses.
- Outline the document as is appropriate for your project and team.

In the next two chapters, I go into more detail about how to write each of the parts outlined.

Creating the Body of the Document

6

With your document well planned, and having conducted initial meetings with the product team and subject matter experts, you're now ready to assemble summaries, diagrams, and process descriptions into a compelling story. You will most likely create two compelling stories: the *current state* and the *future state*. I will also explore the importance of a few types of nonnarrative content like a gap analysis, data specification, and requirements summary.

The current and future states both have very similar, if not identical, structures. Both include an arrangement of elements, most of which I have already covered, similar to the following:

- A short introduction to the main processes of the current state
- A list of nonfunctional requirements and business rules
- A high-level diagram that shows the entire work of the system and how it interacts with other systems (a *context* diagram)
- One or more data flow diagrams (including summaries)
- Process descriptions and requirements for all processes

Is Documenting the Current State Really Necessary?

Use a current state analysis when a manual business process is being automated for the first time, or when an existing system is being substantially changed. A thorough current state analysis captures what is being done, so that the future system will meet the same requirements. If you are working on a completely new process that is now not functioning at all, you may be able skip the current state and go straight to the future state analysis, but in most cases, it's worthwhile to say at least a little about the current state, even if there isn't much to it.

If your project team is very impatient with documentation and strapped for time and resources, you can try to save time with a minimal current state, or leave it out altogether. You may then need to explain more in the future state.

Go Back to the Team

Earlier in the book I described how to gather important stakeholders and ask them to name all the things the system does (its processes), all the players in the processes, all the important data, and all the external interactors. If you have met with all the right stakeholders and identified the processes that they believe are important, you should be able to use this information to sketch out a rough draft of the current state.

Gather all the statements about the system that your stakeholders came up with and separate them according to what the system does now and what they hope the system will do in the future. Take all the statements about what the system does now and try to group them into processes. It is very unlikely you will have enough detail from the simple statements to actually complete data flow diagrams and process descriptions. For that you need to work closely with subject matter experts.

Present Draft Diagrams

Instead, assemble a collection of draft diagrams that will convey the basic scope of the work you propose.

Present your collection of draft diagrams to the project team to find out if they believe that these processes, if fully documented, would capture the requirements of the current system. Now that they can see what happens to the information they give you, encourage the team to give you more and expand the system inventory, checking for missing processes, actors, components, or anything else you discover.

Feel free to add your own elements, particularly about nonfunctional areas such as usability, interface design, maintenance processes, and so on.

A Sample Project Inventory

You can use a variety of different categories that might be meaningful in your project. I find those in the examples that follow to be very common and useful.

Things involved in the current state:
- Operations Staff
- Operations Management
- Customer Transaction Files
- FileTrans

- Shared folder for deliveries
- OFAC database
- Transaction Management System (TMS)

What happens now/accomplishments:

- Matching accounts
- Checking unknown accounts against OFAC
- Handling delivery problems
- Entering transactions in TMS
- Communicating delivery problems to management
- Setting up new accounts
- Reporting suspicious transactions
- Maintaining account data

Inputs you can't change:

- FileTrans file drop
- Format of customer transaction file

Outputs you can't change:

- OFAC queries
- Transaction entry in TMS

Good qualities of how it works now:

- Is done by 5 p.m. EST 90% of the time
- Two operations staff can handle the current transaction volume.
- Transaction fail rate from bad accounts is less than 1%.
- Easy to change process as new screening data becomes available and laws change

Bad qualities of how it works now:

- Depends on knowledge of senior staff
- Can't hire and train staff with sufficient knowledge
- Can't meet expected 50% increase in volume next year
- Although transaction processing is usually done on time, the 10% delay won't be acceptable at higher volumes.

Other things to consider might be security, regulations, more about performance, and so on. For the resources available to this project, I have decided this level is appropriate and the rest I will assume.

The level of detail in current state analysis can vary considerably. In a simple system or a small change to a more complex system, a single high-level data flow diagram may suffice. In a more detailed specification, a complete tabular process description may work better. I discussed this point in the previous chapter.

Consider Context

One of the most important things to consider when documenting the current state is how the system must fit into its environment. Typically, it isn't possible to change what goes into the system. Likewise, other systems may depend on receiving something from the system you are changing or creating. All software must run on hardware and operating systems that cannot be changed, in addition to having to interact with data from a wide variety of external sources. Current state documentation is very effective at capturing and detailing these kinds of requirements.

A context diagram is a very simple type of data flow diagram that reduces the entire system to as few processes as possible, often only one, and shows only the external interactors and data stores. This can be very helpful in finding requirements. In the following diagram, I've represented the entire system as a single process named "Process Orders," which reads orders from three data stores and sends them to the external "Warehouse Systems."

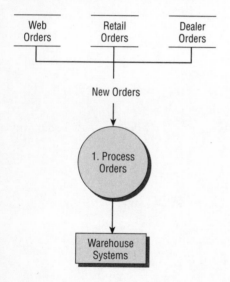

Complete a Single Process

After returning to your group with rough drafts and gathering more details, ask the group to choose the most important process—the one the group would like documented first. This task itself will help the group reach consensus and clarify its priorities. Once the group chooses the process to be documented, have the group choose subject matter experts to provide you with any further details.

For the chosen process, meet as much as necessary with the subject matter experts and create a finished data flow diagram (or diagrams) with all necessary subdiagrams. Complete process descriptions at the level of detail you think appropriate. Choose the most effective structure of text and graphics. Write a summary of the process and include nonfunctional requirements. (You can even write up the same process a few different ways and let the team choose which it likes best.)

Take the finished product back to the team for confirmation on the approach. Seeing the most important process clearly documented will no doubt inspire many new ideas and bring out more information about related processes. Be ready to capture and incorporate everything you learn.

With the approach agreed upon and the processes prioritized, you should be able to work through the rest of the processes faster. As you continue, adjust the number of rounds of review to something the team is comfortable with, but be sure you get the feedback you need. I will discuss the review process in greater detail in a later chapter.

Using Cross-References

Use an automated cross-referencing feature, such as Bookmarks in Microsoft Word, to tag each of your requirements for reuse. I bookmark all the requirements as I go along so I can insert them anywhere in the document and update all the instances at once. Bookmarks are also essential to building requirements summaries and other tables. If you change the source of the bookmark text, all the instances change automatically—a great feature for maintaining the document as requirements change.

Use a prefix such as CS_ (current state) before the requirement number so you can quickly tell that the requirement originated from the current state.

Writing the Future State

The future state describes the stakeholders' consensus on what they believe the system should do in the future. I use the same approach to writing the future state as I described for the current state. Create rough diagrams of a proposed future state and go back to the team for prioritization and help adding details. There are, however, a few issues unique to the future state to bear in mind.

Carrying Requirements Forward

Be sure not to rewrite requirements that were already stated in the current state documentation. This not only saves you work, but enables you to avoid cluttering the project with superfluous or redundant requirements. Instead, use an automated cross-reference to the original requirement. I discussed the Microsoft Word Bookmark feature earlier in this chapter.

Don't Design Solutions

One trap to avoid when documenting a future state is to go beyond stating requirements and to design a solution. In many cases, you may not realize you're designing a solution, but look carefully at your actions and requirements statements. An action should describe only what happens, not *how* it happens. Requirements should focus on the quality of the results and not dictate the results themselves.

For example, "User chooses Open New Account from the File menu," sounds like a simple action, but it actually specifies the name of a new command. Command names should be carefully written and checked against all the other command names in the system, not made up in passing while writing requirements. A better action statement would be, "User operates the system controls to start the New Account process."

Similarly, a requirements statement such as, "Check accounts against OFAC database," is designing the solution. A better statement would be, "Check new accounts for matches in the best available data on suspicious accounts."

I also don't agree with those who design a user interface at the same time as specifying requirements. In my experience, stakeholders focus too much on the aesthetics and usability of the design and lose track of the underlying functionality and requirements. Nail down exactly what must be accomplished at each step and then design the interface. This doesn't mean you can't say anything about the interface in a requirements document. I prefer defining an interface design process as a unique requirement, separate from the process descriptions. "There shall be an interface design process in which prototypes of the interface that meet all functional requirements are presented to a team comprised of one user from each stakeholder group, the product manager, and the technical writer. The designers will modify the design based on feedback from the team until the majority of the team is satisfied."

Statements about solutions belong in functional specifications, not requirements documents. All this said, you should write the document that works for your team, and if certain solutions are essentially predetermined, such as using the OFAC database or a certain command name, go ahead and use them. Don't let this ideology make your document less useful to the team.

Checking for Completeness

Using the kind of data flow diagrams and process descriptions I've been describing makes it a lot easier to find missing requirements. Try to follow your diagrams as a story and missing parts will become obvious. The clearer you make the diagrams, grouping related processes and putting them in the proper order, the easier it becomes to see what's missing.

There is no single way to make sure you have captured every requirement. You should use a variety of techniques, and most important, you should have your work reviewed many times by key stakeholders.

Make sure that all the elements listed by the team before you finished your draft are in some way included in the process descriptions or listed up front as part of the summary, high-level, or nonfunctional requirements.

Look at the inputs and outputs of all processes, not only within single flows, but also in connecting flows and external systems. Make sure that there is an explicit requirement specifying exactly what, when, and how data must be delivered to each process and external. Be sure also to consider data specifications. It may be helpful to create a table and check off the input and output requirements for each process.

Every system takes data from somewhere, does something to it, and puts it somewhere. You can use this very simple analysis to find missing requirements. Look at each type of data and consider if you've explained what it is, how it is obtained or created, how it is used and changed, and where it ends up. You can set up a table for this. The table shouldn't appear in your document, unless you want to put it in an appendix as a credibility builder.

Data Type	Source	Used by Process	Related Requirements	Output(s)
Accounts	Customers	3.1, 3.2, 3.3	CS_FR 3.1, CS_FR 6.2, Data Spec. A.1	TMS
Transactions	Customers	1.1, 1.4		TMS
Customers	Customers	6.3, 7.1	CS_FR 9.3m Data Spec. A.2	Create Account

A quick look at the preceding table shows that we need to provide adequate requirements for Transaction data.

Prototypes

This is a great way of testing the completeness of requirements before actually building functionality. You can use a future state description as a prototype. Create functionality mockups in a graphics program, PowerPoint, or even a prototyping program, that illustrate the important stages of your processes (don't make them look like a finished user interface). Project them on a screen and talk through typical workflows with your team. You may need to go through a few rounds of prototyping because each round uncovers so many new requirements.

It can also be helpful to think of particular people, real or fictional, that play a role in a process or must be satisfied by it. Talk through the processes and consider the needs of those people at each step. Make sure there are requirements ensuring that all those people's needs are met.

Reference Material After the Story

The current state and future state make up the real story of the system to be built and the work to be done. However, there is much important information and supporting material that you should put in the sections after the future state. These will vary considerably depending on the project. In fast-moving projects with light documentation, it may be best to leave them out entirely, or include only the data specification. Trust your own judgment but also include the team in your decision of what to include or leave out.

Refer to the sample outline in a previous chapter for suggestions on where to place this material.

Gap Analysis

A gap analysis extracts and explains the key differences between the current and future states. If the team has something important to say about the new requirements in general, the gap analysis can sometimes provide the right place to say it. A gap analysis can be a good place to go into more detail about the reasons behind a requirement than is possible in the process descriptions or the executive summary.

If you've done a good job of carrying requirements forward, the gap analysis should almost write itself. The future state requirements represent what the system does not do now that the team wants it to do in the future. If you bookmarked the requirements as you went along, it's an easy matter to assemble the current state requirements in a column on the left, with corresponding future state requirements in the middle, and then a column to the right for comments about the key differences and possibly the benefits.

Current Requirement	Related Future Requirement	Benefits
CS_FR 3.2: Operations Staff alerts Transaction team management by phone and e-mail if the transactions do not arrive by 3:30 p.m. EST.	**FS_FR 4.1:** Delivery process monitors drop folder and begins processing immediately upon receipt of a complete transaction file.	No manual activity is required to begin processing. Delivery problems generate notification automatically.
CS_FR 3.3: Operations Staff immediately informs FileTrans when the transaction file is not present or is unreadable and requests correction and recovery time.	**FS_FR 4.2:** Delivery process notifies FileTrans and Transaction team management if no files have arrived by 3:00 p.m. EST.	

Requirements Summaries

Requirements summaries are simple lists of requirements organized in various helpful ways. If you've properly bookmarked all your requirements, generating and maintaining lists are easy. Probably the most helpful list is a simple, comprehensive one. Put all of the requirements in numerical order.

So far we've used processes as the primary way to capture and organize requirements. As the project continues, it is very helpful to look at different groups of requirements in various logical groupings. I've made a big point about not diagramming or designing components of the new system, but at this point, you should consider components and find the requirements associated with them.

Review the process descriptions and make a list of all the entities with which you would like to associate requirements. Now go back through the list of requirements and match them to the components to make subgroupings of requirements.

In the example lists that follow, notice that the same requirements appear on more than one list. Requirements can be involved with many components and it's helpful to see all of the requirements associated with each component. It's also helpful to see requirements associated with other entities, such as a team, a piece of hardware, a report, or any other grouping you find useful.

FileTrans requirements:

CS_FR 3.1: FileTrans must deliver all transaction files for daily processing to the transaction file drop folder by 3 p.m. EST.

CS_NFR 3.1: FileTrans must respond within 30 minutes to file delivery queries with a recovery time estimate.

Transaction team management:

NFR 3.2: Transaction team management must respond to FileTrans issues when FileTrans has not responded or is unreachable for 30 minutes.

Business rules:

BZR 3.1: All transactions must be between known entities and accounts that have been screened for any record of improper activities.

BZR 5.1: New accounts must be confirmed manually by two staff members in accordance with MegaCorp Account Management Policy and Procedure.

Operations staff:

CS_FR 3.2: Operations Staff alerts Transaction team management by phone and e-mail if the transactions do not arrive by 3:30 p.m. EST.

CS_FR 3.3: Operations Staff immediately informs FileTrans when the transaction file is not present or unreadable and requests correction and recovery time.

CS_FR: 3.3: Operations Staff alerts Transaction team management if FileTrans is unreachable for 30 minutes.

CS_FR: 3.4: The Account Screening Database is maintained with daily feeds from firm-approved services monitoring suspicious accounts.

CS_FR 3.5: Accounts for the buyer and seller of each transaction have been identified and cleared for compliance with company transaction guidelines.

CS_FR. 3.6: Unknown accounts that have no record of suspicious activity are held and researched for new account creation.

BZR 3.1: All transactions must be between known entities and accounts that have been screened by OFAC for any record of improper activities.

Account Screening Process:
BZR 3.1: All transactions must be between known entities and accounts that have been screened by OFAC for any record of improper activities.

CS_FR. 3.6: Unknown accounts that have no record of suspicious activity are held and researched for new account creation.

CS_FR 7.1: OFAC query for unknown accounts must look for matches by first and last names (including two-character differences), company matches, sovereignty matches, transactional matches, and product matches.

CS_FR: 3.4: The Account Screening Database is maintained with daily feeds from firm-approved services monitoring suspicious accounts.

Delivery Process:
CS_FR 3.2: Operations Staff alerts Transaction team management by phone and e-mail if the transactions do not arrive by 3:30 p.m. EST.

CS_FR 3.3: Operations Staff immediately informs FileTrans when the transaction file is not present or unreadable and requests correction and recovery time.

CS_FR: 3.3: Operations Staff alerts Transaction team management if FileTrans is unreachable for 30 minutes.

Data Specifications

Data specifications belong in an appendix, but they are a vital part of the document. The data specification supplies all the cumbersome detail that you don't want to bog down your process descriptions. Data specifications can be lengthy, often longer than process descriptions. I once wrote a requirements document that comprised only 10 pages of process descriptions and over 125 pages of data specifications. Don't think this means you can sometimes skip the process descriptions. The data alone can never tell the whole story.

For a requirements document, data specification should explain the meaning and content of the data. This may require including calculations that look like programming code, or simple English definitions. Do not supply character counts or data type (alpha, binary, numeric, and so on). You and the team must choose what is appropriate for your project.

The following example explains the data in a spreadsheet that is to be automated. The spreadsheet does many calculations on the data, and as part of the current state analysis, it was necessary to explain all the calculations.

Primary Detail Field Name	Derivation	Current Source
Grade (AAA, BB, LQ, Non-Investment Grade)	If UPLOAD:INTERNAL_RTG ≥ BBB then "AAA" else "Non-Investment Grade"	Extracted from XYS to the DOWNLOAD worksheet
Deal Type (*Relationship or Event*)	Manually entered	**Available in XYS as Loan Purpose Type, not currently imported
Deal Status No value is visible in current records—only for grouping	If DOWNLOAD:TRADE DATE BAL > 0 then "Live Deal" else "Flat Deal"	Extracted from XYS to the DOWNLOAD worksheet
Bilateral Position Indicator Simple binary indicator	E-mail (available in XYS) Đ = Bilateral position	**Available in XYS as Loan Purpose Type, not currently imported
Held by (*Company*)	Assign value based on value of DOWNLOAD: BRANCH. If "MXSFP" then "C" If "MXSFI" then " " (Blank means NY) If "Utah" then "U"	Extracted from XYS to the DOWNLOAD worksheet
Deal	= DOWNLOAD:DEAL	Extracted from XYS to the DOWNLOAD worksheet
Coverage Officer	Manually entered	**Available in XYS, not currently imported.
Industry Silo	Manually entered	**Available in XYS, not currently imported

Primary Detail Field Name	Derivation	Current Source
Issue CCY	= DOWNLOAD:FACILITY CURR	Extracted from XYS to the DOWNLOAD worksheet
Outstanding CCY	= DOWNLOAD:GL CURR	Extracted from XYS to the DOWNLOAD worksheet
Issue Date	Manually entered	**Available in XYS, not currently imported

Report Specifications

Your system may be required to generate specific reports. You can specify exactly what the report should include, how calculations should be made, how data should be grouped, and anything else about the report, short of the design itself.

I find the following format effective.

< Title>

< Date>

\<Group by Division >

\<Product Group> (Housewares)

\<Group by Product ID>

\<Display the following tabular fields>

Product ID	Int ID	Long Name	Starting Inventory	Closing	Net Revenue	Carry Cost	Profit
\<Subtotals by Division>		Long Name	Starting Inventory	Closing	Net Revenue	Carry Cost	Profit
\<Totals, all records in the worksheet>				Closing	Net Revenue	Carry Cost	Profit

Summary

We've now covered several important points about assembling the final document and many of its sections:

- Work with the project team to build the project inventory, refine your process, set priorities, and ensure you are providing what is necessary and most useful.
- Assemble logically grouped data flow diagrams, process descriptions, and summaries to form the body of the document.
- Organize the current and future states to show how the system works now and how you would like it to work in the future.
- Check for completeness by examining inputs and outputs and various groupings of requirements, and also by simply reading your work as a story.
- Add nonnarrative sections such as data specifications, report specifications, gap analysis, and requirements summaries to support narrative content and keep it clutter free.

With the body of the document reasonably under control, you're ready to start work on what could be the most important part of the document, the executive summary.

And Finally, the Beginning

7

When all the detailed content of your document is essentially complete, you're ready to seize your reader's attention and make your points with a clear and forceful executive summary. To write a great executive summary, combine your talent for telling stories with your rigorous analysis skills. Condense the conclusions of the project team to a very few brief recommendations and *put them first*, even if you may be uncomfortable strongly recommending something before building a case.

We often start documents with a lot of unnecessary background information. Have you heard this before?

> The issues surrounding account screening require thorough and thoughtful analysis. With the advent of money laundering issues in the wake of the increase in drug trafficking during the 1990s, as well as concern about the global flows of capital in support of terrorist organizations after the tragedies of 9/11, the firm has become concerned that greater efforts must be made in prevention of transactions with unverified counterparties. After reaching out to partners around the firm in an extensive effort involving stakeholders at every level of management, from associates to managing directors to clients, the Transaction Processing Improvement team (TPI) has initiated a groundbreaking process of recommendation for the next generation of ... "

Please wake me up when we hit some information.

Like the first few pages of a good novel, the executive summary should be immediately compelling and introduce the ideas that will be developed later. Unlike a novel, you should assume no one is going to read any other chapter.

Use the executive summary to explain the entire body of work, discuss its fundamental benefits, and define the problem at hand. Also be sure to build credibility for the process by which you arrived at these conclusions and show that the team addressed common concerns.

The executive summary should make very clear what the project team wants done in one to five pages, depending on the size of the project. Your very impatient readers should not have to dig through the entire document to get the basic idea. Most of your readers will read *only* the executive summary and perhaps briefly skim a few other sections that interest them.

The executive summary functions almost as a stand-alone document. It is a complete whole, supported by the detail of the rest of the document. Remove it from the document entirely and you should be able to use it as a *vision and scope* document.

The parts of an executive summary vary somewhat depending on the nature of the project and the conventions of each organization, but the following parts are common to most:

- Recommendations
- High-level diagram
- Problem and context
- Requirements gathering process
- General considerations
- Scope

One thing you may expect that you don't see here is anything about schedules, cost, or resources available. In this book I focus narrowly on expressing what project stakeholders need and want. It's a good idea to roughly quantify the benefits of your recommendations or to point out the costs of some of the problems you hope to solve, but this is not the place to get into a laborious analysis of the project cost and schedule. You can't address cost, resources, and schedule without proposing a specific solution implementation, and doing this undermines the requirements gathering process. Save cost estimates for when you are proposing a specific project plan.

Recommendations

The end result of all your requirements gathering should be a few summary recommendations. Each single recommendation may represent a group of requirements and functionality, or it may represent only one. If the recommendations are not obvious from the work done so far, reconvene the project team and go through the requirements summary to reach consensus on what few things you want to say first. The list should be between three and seven items, but not more than 10. The list should include the most critical functional requirements (what the system will do), and some indication of success and performance indicators (how well the system will do what it does). Depending on what you are proposing, you may want to include organizational requirements (new staff, management, or a support group).

Be sure to summarize without being too general. You can't explain every detail, but you can write a statement that really means something. Recall what we learned earlier about specific as opposed to general language. Also remember that requirements and recommendations should include clear and measurable success criteria.

Executive summaries can bring out the nervous generalizer in all of us, leading to jargon-ridden, important-sounding but meaningless statements so common in modern business communication. It may be hard for you to state something so bluntly. Plain, clear recommendations are uncommon in our usual communication.

Consider the following paragraph:

> We recommend automating the account delivery and screening process to provide state-of-the-art performance and industry-standard functionality to what is now a cumbersome manual process. Our goals are to minimize impact to upstream and downstream systems, maximize real-time transaction throughput, and create reusable technology objects, while delivering critical functionality to underserved operations staff.

Like a bad political speech, this statement uses a lot of empty phrases such as "state-of-the-art-performance" and "maximize real-time throughput." It sounds impressively technical, but makes no commitments and does not define the work to be done. We use these kinds of phrases to sound important and to cover up that we don't know what to say and would prefer not to be specific about what we're going to do.

Compare the previous statement to the following:

> The Transactions Processing Improvement team recommends automating transaction delivery, account screening, and transaction entry to automatically accept newly delivered electronic transaction files, report delivery problems, verify that accounts are valid, screen unknown accounts, restructure transaction data, and import it directly to the Transaction Management System (TMS). The system must search for unknown accounts in the latest available U.S. government listings of suspicious entities and jurisdictions. The new system should be capable of handling a projected transaction growth of four times the current volume with no increase in processing time, staffing, or manual effort above current levels.

In contrast to the previous example, this paragraph is specific about what the team believes should be built (transaction delivery, account screening, and so on). It also provides a measurable performance and scalability goal (handling projected fourfold transaction growth). It does not use empty, popular phrases such as "state-of-the-art."

It is, however, hard to take in all the detail in a single paragraph like this, and the recommendations could certainly use even more specifics. Bullet points are more effective when you need to include more detail. A page-number reference to the process description for each recommendation is another very effective addition. Even if the reader doesn't look at the reference, knowing that the information is so easily available builds credibility.

See how the same material might look in a bulleted structure:

The Transactions Processing Improvement team recommends automating transaction delivery, account screening, and transaction entry to accomplish the following:

- Automatically process newly delivered transaction files immediately upon delivery and enter exception-free or "conforming" transactions into TMS within one minute of delivery. (page ref)
- Report delivery problems to team management, customers, and delivery vendors, according to service level agreements with delivery vendors. (page ref)
- Verify that accounts involved in transactions are of known customers. (page ref)
- Automatically match unknown accounts to the latest available U.S. government listings of suspicious entities and jurisdictions, producing reports of near matches for manual review and reducing manual effort required by half. (page ref)
- Send unknown screened accounts to the shared folder for New Account Setup and immediately generate e-mail to Customer Service. (page ref)
- Restructure the incoming data to the Transaction Processing System order structure. (page ref)
- Scale to handle projected transaction growth of four times the current volume with no increase in processing time, staffing, or manual effort above current levels. (page ref)

A High-Level Diagram

A basic high-level diagram can quickly give your readers a useful view of the system. You can put it right after the recommendations with a short introduction, as follows:

The diagram that follows shows a high-level view of the system's processes.

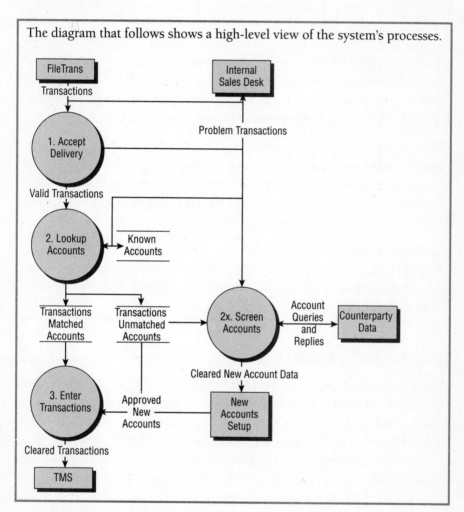

Problem and Context Statement

Follow the recommendations with an explanation of the problem the team hopes to solve and the broader context. Describe the problem to be solved and the overall operating environment. Point out what functions depend on this system and also upon what the system depends.

In the current system, electronically delivered transaction files are viewed on paper or on-screen and then manually screened and entered into TMS. This process remains from when all transactions were delivered from the sales office on paper or by telephone. The operations team currently does an admirable job of keeping up with the increasing flow of transactions while maintaining the firm's account screening standards, but there is broad consensus in the project team that the operations group cannot expand its capacity to keep up with the projected business growth. In particular, the account screening process is entirely manual and there is significant risk of overlooking a suspicious new account or failing to notice an illegal trading pattern. New staff cannot be trained rapidly enough to perform all the functions of the current staff.

The current manual system performs a critical function in validating accounts and enforcing anti–money laundering policies. Roughly 30% of the firm's revenue depends on the timely and accurate processing of these transactions. Additionally, given that the transaction data is already entered in a structured system, it is wasteful and unnecessary to manually reenter it into TMS.

Roughly half of new accounts result from electronically delivered transaction files. For external transactions, the system depends on the vendor FileTrans to securely deliver transaction files. Internal files are manually copied to a shared folder.

Requirements Process

Follow recommendations with a brief statement of the process that created the requirements. You want readers who are completely unfamiliar with the project to know that the work represents a methodical, credible and collaborative effort, not just the author's. Again, use some precise details to explain the process. Explain which stakeholders contributed to the document and something about the process of creating and reviewing the document:

To create this document a team comprised of key stakeholders from operations staff, accounts staff, IT Infrastructure, IT development, front office sales, and senior management met in various groupings over the course of several weeks. (For a complete list of participants, see "Project Stakeholder and Team Members" in Appendix X.) In addition to providing information, reviewers have also approved the written requirements and recommendations and reviewed this entire document.

General Considerations

This is a loosely defined section that provides a place to discuss and analyze issues, risks, dependencies, or anything else that might affect the project. These typically include important general concerns that don't fit neatly into requirements or recommendations, or statements of considerations made that might not be otherwise apparent. Be careful not to include too much—two or three paragraphs are best. Try to anticipate and answer the main questions that will arise from the recommendations. Imagine a senior manager smugly putting down the document after skimming the bulleted recommendations and saying, "OK, but have you thought of … "

Operations staff has expressed a general concern that too many anomalies arise in transactions to effectively automate screening and account entry, and that ultimately many judgments that cannot be automated have to be made about whether to proceed with transaction settlement. The current manual process has been an important risk and quality control checkpoint in the operations workflow.

The project team agrees with these concerns but believes that automating the simplest tasks (delivery issues, data entry, routine account matching, etc.) can actually improve the current staff's abilities to handle anomalies and apply better judgment where necessary. The team does advise that the new system not attempt to automate decisions about account screening if there is not an exact match.

The team has also considered the possibility that the transaction rate will not increase at currently projected levels. Even at current rates, operations staff is often required to work overtime to keep up. If the amount of time spent with delivery problems and account screening could be reduced by half (as specified in our requirements), staff would be available for handling other tasks (such as month-end closing and new account setup) and would not need to work overtime. Overtime now amounts to roughly 15% of the operations staff cost.

Scope

The scope defines what work will be included in the project. Many projects fail because they take on too much. It is certainly tempting to take on all the problems at hand once work gets underway, but it's vital that you state up front what the project will and will not address. Without a clearly written scope, work can easily meander into new areas, suffering what is aptly described as "scope creep." Scope creep drains resources from a project and distracts from the accomplishment of core goals.

In defining the scope of work, consider the most critical problems, the probable time and resources available (even though this is not a project plan), and the degree of control that the project stakeholders have over the elements of the problem. The scope statement in a requirements document is most important for expressing the team's priorities. The scope will likely change as the project plan evolves, but it is important to know the team's priorities at the start of the project.

You may need to explain some points in more detail, but I prefer simple lists of what is in the project and what is out, like the following:

The project will address the following areas:

- Transaction delivery (handling files once they are delivered to Operations shared drives)
- Account screening
- Delivery of new account data to customer service
- Data structuring
- Data entry in TMS

The project will not address the following potentially related areas:

- Delivery processes (by FileTrans, other vendors, or internal processes)
- New account setup procedures
- TMS order processing
- TMS data structures

Other Potential Sections

There can be many other sections in an executive summary, but don't include any of them without a specific reason and meaningful content. Many organizations use templates or have conventions for executive summaries. In most cases you can adapt the content I've discussed so far to fit these templates. Be careful about including sections that lead the document into material that you cannot support. In particular, be careful not to make the executive summary into a project plan that includes schedules, cost estimates, resource requests, and so on. A requirements document should be a simple, focused, detailed statement of what is required in a proposed body of work. After studying the requirements, the project team and management should agree on what work is to be undertaken, and then the project manager can create a detailed project plan.

Many senior managers and organizations ask for a combination of requirements and a project proposal in the same document. While this approach undermines the effectiveness of both efforts, I understand you may have no choice but to comply. If you must do both things at once, be mindful of each separate purpose and try not to let implementation concerns disrupt the requirements gathering process.

Some common sections in executive summaries include the following:

- **Key Performance Indicators (or Success Criteria):** These are specific metrics for measuring the success of the system and project, better suited to a project plan. Well-written recommendations should include sufficiently measureable means of gauging performance and overall success, so don't include this section unless necessary for another reason.
- **Risk and Benefits:** If the document must convince wary managers to proceed with the work, use a table comparing specific risks to benefits.
- **References:** If the work refers to many other documents created for the project or by the organization, it may help to list them.
- **Roles and Responsibilities:** This material is much better suited to an appendix, but it can be of vital interest on some projects.

A Complete Example

It's helpful to see a complete executive summary, including all the parts I've described so far in order. Notice that the first section is just called "executive summary" and not "Recommendations."

Executive Summary

The Transactions Processing Improvement team recommends automating transaction delivery, account screening, and transaction entry to accomplish the following:

- Automatically process newly delivered transaction files immediately upon delivery and enter exception-free or "conforming" transactions into TMS within one minute of delivery. (page ref)
- Report delivery problems to team management, customers, and delivery vendors, according to service level agreements with delivery vendors. (page ref)
- Verify that accounts involved in transactions are of known customers. (page ref)
- Automatically match unknown accounts to the latest available U.S. government listings of suspicious entities and jurisdictions, producing reports of near matches for manual review, reducing manual effort required by half. (page ref)
- Send unknown screened accounts to the shared folder for New Account Setup and immediately generate e-mail to Customer Service. (page ref)
- Restructure the incoming data to the Transaction Processing System order structure. (page ref)
- Scale to handle projected transaction growth of four times the current volume with no increase in processing time, staffing, or manual effort above current levels. (page ref)

The diagram that follows on the opposite page shows a high-level view of the system's processes.

Problem and Context

In the current system, electronically delivered transaction files are viewed on paper or on-screen and then manually screened and entered into TMS. This process is a holdover from when all transactions were delivered from the sales office on paper or by telephone. The operations team currently does an admirable job of keeping up with the increasing flow of transactions while maintaining the firm's account screening standards, but there is broad consensus in the project team that the operations group cannot expand its capacity to keep up with the projected business growth. In particular, the account screening process is entirely manual and there is significant risk

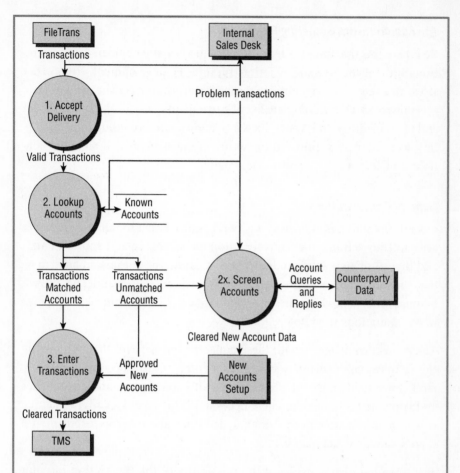

of overlooking a suspicious new account or failing to notice an illegal trading pattern. New staff cannot be trained rapidly enough to perform all the functions of the current staff.

The current manual system performs a critical function in validating accounts and enforcing anti–money laundering policies. Roughly 30% of the firm's revenue depends on the timely and accurate processing of these transactions. Additionally, given that the transaction data is already entered in a structured system, it is wasteful and unnecessary to manually reenter it into TMS.

Roughly half of new accounts result from electronically delivered transaction files. For external transactions, the system depends on the vendor FileTrans to securely deliver transaction files. Internal files are manually copied to a shared folder.

The Requirements Gathering Process

To create this document, a team comprising key stakeholders from operations staff, accounts staff, IT infrastructure, IT development, front office sales, and senior management met in various groupings over the course of several weeks. (For a complete list of participants, see "Project stakeholder and team members" in Appendix X.) In addition to providing information, reviewers have also approved the written requirements and recommendations and reviewed this entire document.

General Considerations

Operations staff has expressed a general concern that too many anomalies arise in transactions to effectively automate screening and account entry, and that ultimately many judgments that cannot be automated have to be made about whether to proceed with transaction settlement. The current manual process has been an important risk and quality control checkpoint in the operations workflow.

The project team agrees with these concerns but believes that automating the simplest tasks (delivery issues, data entry, routine account matching, etc.) can actually improve the current staff's abilities to handle anomalies and apply better judgment where necessary. The team does advise that the new system not attempt to automate decisions about account screening if there is not an exact match.

The team has also considered the possibility of the transaction rate not increasing at currently projected levels. Even at current rates, operational staff is often required to work overtime to keep up. If the amount of time spent with delivery problems and account screening could be reduced by half (as specified in our requirements), staff would be available for handling other tasks (such as month-end closing and new account setup) and would not need to work overtime. Overtime now amounts to roughly 15% of the operations staff cost.

Scope

The project will address the following areas:

- Transaction delivery (handling files once they are delivered to Operations shared drives)

- Account screening
- Delivery of new account data to customer service
- Data structuring
- Data entry in TMS

The project will not address the following potentially related areas:

- Delivery processes (by FileTrans, other vendors, or internal processes)
- New account setup procedures
- TMS order processing
- TMS data structures

Summary

The executive summary is the most important part of the document. It must forcefully present the project team's recommendations and explain enough about what went into them to win the support of key decision makers. When you write your executive summary:

- Put clear and detailed recommendations early in the executive summary. Use bullet points to make the recommendations stand out.
- Use a high-level diagram to quickly provide an overview of the system.
- Define the key problem and the broader context of the problem.
- Explain the process that produced the recommendations.
- Provide any general material and discussion that is important to understanding the recommendations.
- Define the scope of the project.
- Do not include cost estimates, resource requests, schedule, or any other detailed project management content.

    In the next chapter, I explain the reviewing process, reusing material from the requirements document as the project develops, and maintaining the document through a system's life cycle.

Reviewing, Reusing, and Maintenance

8

This chapter describes the process of reviewing and maintaining the entire document after it is complete and also discusses some possibilities for harvesting the content in later stages of development to create functional specifications and test plans, and for basic project management.

Review Cycles

As you work, process by process, section by section, you should share your work with key team members for feedback. Once the entire document is done, distribute review copies to the entire team and allow them enough time to provide feedback. Your work is not complete until it has been thoroughly reviewed.

I also recommend testing the document on a select group outside the project team, if possible, before circulating it more broadly.

It is impossible to produce polished work without external review. There will always be embarrassing typos, wrong assumptions, incorrect details, and many other corrections that are not apparent to you, the author.

Reviewing documentation can be tedious work, and most people don't like to do it. When reviewers are not responsive, you should assess the strength of the story elements in the document. Reviewers are more motivated when the executive summary is forceful and makes clear recommendations, and all of the data flow diagrams have compelling introductions that tie each section to the overall story. Also consider making your diagrams more comprehensible by grouping related processes and annotating.

If you are still not getting a meaningful response from reviewers, have a review meeting. Schedule about two hours and bring snacks. Read the document aloud and encourage discussion. It is always most difficult to get feedback on what is *not* in the document. Talking through the processes can often turn up missing steps, incomplete data, and many other missing elements.

Sign Off

Once a document has been reviewed, I strongly recommend going through some sort of formal acceptance process. You can come up with a process that is appropriate for your organization. A simple signed cover sheet can suffice. What you want to obtain is a clear record that the requirements as described in the document were formally accepted by the key stakeholders in the project. If you are working with external developers, or if you are an external developer yourself (or represent one), a signed requirements document is vital when you begin work on a project. Without a signed document, you are vulnerable to changes in the project scope and the addition of requirements that can send a project off course.

What Happens Next

With a requirements document completed and accepted, the material begins its useful life. In some rapid development processes, developers start creating working software before requirements documentation is done (if it is done at all). In other processes, the developers or a requirements analyst will study the requirements and write a proposal for a specific solution that meets as many of the requirements as possible.

Application Proposals

The proposal includes high-level technical-implementation concepts and usually some estimates of resources required, costs, and schedules. Ideally, the proposal systematically addresses the written requirements and may even include many of the same diagrams and tables.

An application proposal should explain the technical details to the extent that an IT manager would need to know to assess the viability of the approach. It may describe the types of technology to be deployed, such as database platforms, programming languages, hardware, and so on. An application proposal should also describe the basic architecture of the system. It may be possible to reuse some of the data flow diagrams created for the requirements document, but it will probably also be necessary to show a component view.

I recommend including the complete requirements summary and linking each requirement to a proposed solution, or to an explanation of why the requirement will not be met.

Functional Specifications

A functional specification is documentation by and for engineers, preferably created with help from a technical writer. The functional specification (or "spec" as it's more commonly known) explains how all the parts are made and how they function together. It usually includes many component architecture diagrams and detailed descriptions of how the components are built, or coded. Some specs explain functionality at the code level and show important parts of the code, or at least name all the important code elements (functions, classes, methods, and so on). Specs often include an Application Program Interface (API) that describes the programming elements that components within or outside the application use to send and receive data and commands.

A functional spec has a much smaller audience than a requirements document, comprising mainly the development team itself. When making assumptions of technical knowledge, or system- or environment-specific details, the authors should consider future members of the team who may not know as much as they do.

The functional specification can make good use of the process diagrams you created, and also the requirements summaries organized by component. For each section in the functional spec that explains how a component will be built, the requirements for that component should be copied from the requirements document.

Test Plans

A test plan defines procedures for evaluating whether an application has met the documented requirements. Test plans can vary widely depending on the size and nature of the application, the skills of the testing staff, the complexity of the environment, and many other factors. An in-depth discussion of testing is well beyond the scope of this book, but from a requirements perspective, there are some basic approaches valid for any testing.

Make sure that for at least the most critical requirements, you document a testing procedure that should produce the documented success criteria of the requirement. For example, consider the requirement, "The system shall detect transactions involving unknown account numbers and prevent them from being entered in the Transaction Management System." A test script for this requirement might go something like this:

1. Create a test transaction file that includes transactions in which either both parties are known accounts, one party is known and the other is unknown, or both are unknown.

2. Copy the test file to the drop folder in the test environment and wait 30 seconds for the file to process.
3. Check TMS to see if the transaction between known parties was entered.
4. Check the Pending OFAC file for the remaining two transactions.

Test is successful if all transactions are in the expected places.

Create scripts like this for every important requirement.

Managing Requirements Through the Project Life Cycle

Regardless of how material in the requirements document is reused, the project manager should use the material, and the requirements summaries in particular, to make sure that the project actually meets the documented requirements.

Managing requirements through the life cycle of a project is a major area of study. There is a wealth of advice available in several books: *Managing Software Requirements*, by Dean Leffingwell and Don Widrig (Addison-Wesley, 2003), and *Software Requirements* by Karl Wiegers (Microsoft Press, 2003) are two of the best.

I recommend at the very least taking the requirements out of your requirements summary table and putting them into some sort of structured data-management tool: a spreadsheet may be adequate, a database for larger projects, or perhaps an automated requirements-management tool. Use the structured data to track that status of requirements as the project evolves.

Requirements often change as a product evolves and new issues arise. It's important to maintain your requirements so that they remain a meaningful and effective management tool throughout the development process. Changes in requirements may also change the narratives you've written. It's very likely you'll reuse the content you've created, so it's wise to keep the entire requirements document up-to-date as requirements change. This will make the next version much easier to write.

Maintaining Requirements After the Application Is in Production

A requirements document should be a *living* document, meaning that it should continue to be revised through a system's entire life cycle. A requirements document is an important record of the thought process that went into creating the system. As a system matures, it is very valuable to see how the decisions stand up to tests of production and time.

Requirements documents sometimes protect both developers and management when a system falls short of expectations. When development is outsourced, requirements documents sometimes provide the evidence of any breach of contract. If users aren't happy but developers can show that they met all of the requirements, management must learn how to improve its requirements process to avoid future disappointments. If management can show that developers did not meet requirements, there can be a basis for reworking the product.

It's not unheard of to write requirements documents for systems after they've been in production for a long time. If no development is planned, you can write a document with only current state explanations.

Summary

It is critical to obtain a thorough review of the requirements document from the most important stakeholders. Remember that:

- It is impossible to create a useful and polished document without at least one thorough review.
- If reviewers are not responsive, you may not have made your document into a sufficiently compelling story. Look again at the executive summary and consider a stronger start; also look at summary introductions and see if they tie each part to the overall story.

A strong requirements documents supports the full life cycle of a project, including the following:

- Test plans
- Basic project management (requirements tracking)
- Technical proposals and functional specs
- A record of the process and the decisions of the project team

Long after the team members have moved on, the requirements document can still tell the story of the project.

Software Requirements Document Template

The template that follows is useful as a starting point for your documents. All the material has been covered elsewhere in the book. The template merely lays out all the recommended sections in order with some brief explanations. I have described other potential sections elsewhere in the book, but these are the ones I really believe in.

Executive Summary

Write the project team's fundamental recommendations, stated as bulleted requirements for the solution (see Chapter 7, "And Finally, the Beginning," for an example of a complete executive summary with content).

Problem and Context

Describe the problem to be solved and the overall operating environment. Point out what functions depend on this system and also on what the system depends.

The Requirements Gathering Process

Describe the process that created the requirements. Show that the work is the outcome of a methodical, credible, and collaborative effort, and not the author's alone. Explain which stakeholders contributed to the document, and something about the process of creating and reviewing the document.

General Considerations

Analyze the issues, risks, dependencies, or anything else that might affect the project. Try to anticipate and answer the main questions that will arise from the recommendations. Be careful not to include too much; two or three paragraphs are best.

Scope

List what processes the project will and will not address. The scope statement must express the team's priorities. Consider the most critical problems, the probable time and resources available, and the degree of control that the project stakeholders have over the elements of the problem.

Use simple lists of what is in the project and what is out:

> *The project will address the following processes:*

> *The project will not address the following potentially related processes:*

Current State

Summarize the main processes of the current system, working in how the problems stated in the executive summary are evident.

Follow the summary with a high-level diagram showing the entire system.

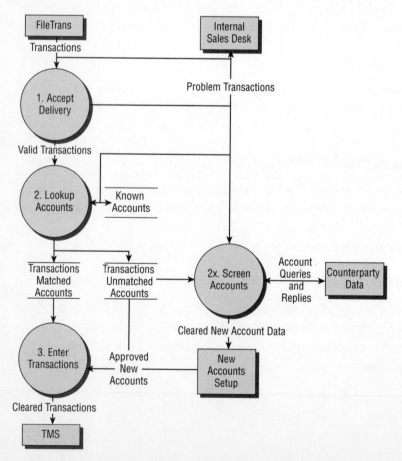

Follow the picture with tables for each of the processes in the diagram. (For more details and examples of content see Chapter 4, "Explaining Processes and Finding Requirements.")

The Exact Name and Number of Process	
Success Criteria	The essential successful result of the process and how exactly to identify and measure it
Started by	The precondition required to begin the process, usually a triggering event. Depending on the type of process, this can also include the data inputs
Results of	The end state of the process, including all data outputs, environment changes, and other products of the process that may not be a direct part of the success criteria
Elements of	The entities involved in the process, including technical components such as servers and software, but also people or groups
Actions	The series of events or steps that comprise the successful completion of the process, including exceptions to the successful sequence
Requirements	The exact functions or conditions that must exist or operate in a certain way in order for the success criteria of the process to be met.
Notes	

Repeat this table structure for each process in the data flow diagram.

If you need to explain a process in more detail than is possible in a single table, break it into a subprocess and create a subdiagram, numbering the process with the number of the top-level process and then a decimal number as shown in the figure that follows.

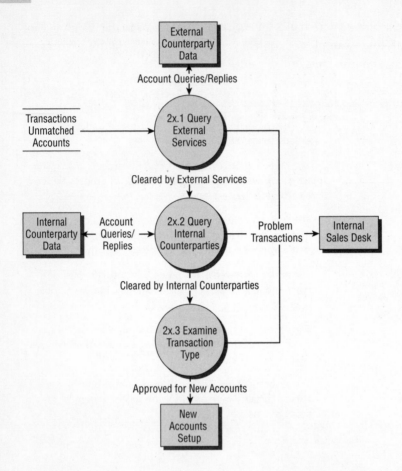

Follow a subdiagram with the same process-description tables shown already.

A Less Formal Structure

Optionally, you can improve readability by rewriting the content of your tables as short prose paragraphs. You can abbreviate further with integrated graphics and text, leaving out a lot of detail, as shown in the figure that follows.

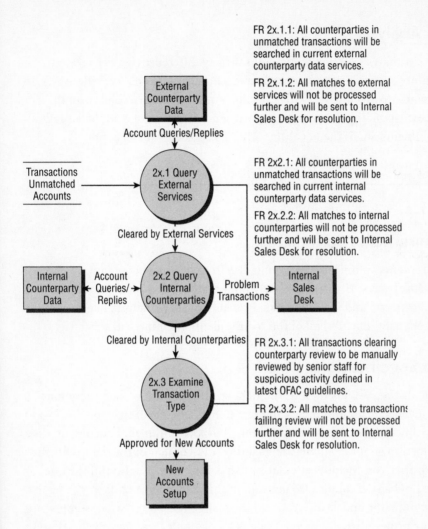

FR 2x.1.1: All counterparties in unmatched transactions will be searched in current external counterparty data services.

FR 2x.1.2: All matches to external services will not be processed further and will be sent to Internal Sales Desk for resolution.

FR 2x2.1: All counterparties in unmatched transactions will be searched in current internal counterparty data services.

FR 2x.2.2: All matches to internal counterparties will not be processed further and will be sent to Internal Sales Desk for resolution.

FR 2x.3.1: All transactions clearing counterparty review to be manually reviewed by senior staff for suspicious activity defined in latest OFAC guidelines.

FR 2x.3.2: All matches to transactions faililng review will not be processed further and will be sent to Internal Sales Desk for resolution.

Future State

Structure the future state exactly the same as the current state. Only the content is different. The future state requirements represent what the system does not do now that the team wants it to do in the future, so you should describe the system to reflect those requirements.

Gap Analysis

Use a gap analysis section to highlight the key differences between the current and future states. If you bookmarked requirements as you went along, it's an easy matter to assemble the current state requirements in a column on the left, with corresponding future state requirements on the right, and then a column for comments about the key differences and possibly the benefits.

Current Requirement	Related Future Requirement	Benefits

Requirements Summaries

Requirements summaries are simple lists of requirements organized in various helpful ways. If you've properly bookmarked all your requirements, it's easy to generate and maintain lists. Probably the most helpful list is a simple, comprehensive one. Put all of the requirements in numerical order.

Data Specifications

Define all the systems data in the data specification (or "data dictionary"). The data specification supplies all the cumbersome detail that you don't want to bog down your process descriptions. For a requirements document, data specification should explain the meaning and content of the data. This may require that you include calculations that look like programming code, or simple English definitions. Do not supply character counts or data type (alpha, binary, numeric, and so on). You and the team must choose what is important for your project. The following table is an example. You may need different columns in yours.

Element Name	Derivation	Current Source
Grade		
(AAA, BB, LQ, Non-Investment Grade)	If UPLOAD:INTERNAL_ RTG ≥ BBB then "AAA" else "Non-Investment Grade"	Extracted from XYS to the DOWNLOAD worksheet

Report Specifications

Specify exactly what required reports should include, how calculations should be made, how data should be grouped, and anything else about the report, short of the design itself.

The following format can be effective.

< Title>
< Date>
<Group by >
<Element Name> (Value)
<Display the following tabular fields>

element	element	element	element	element	calculation	calculation
Subtotal						
Total						

Version History

At the end of the document, maintain a version history that shows what major changes were made in each version, the date, and who made them.

Index

levels of hierarchy, 46
names and numbers, 62
overview of, 61–62
prioritizing and completing single,
  100–101
results of, 63
sizing, 50–51
structuring with prose-based approach,
  76–78
structuring with tabular approach,
  73–76
in summary and detail diagrams, 43–45
summary review, 81
writing success criteria, 62–63
project team
building rapport with, 84–85
completing single process using,
  100–101
creating body of document with
  information from, 98
Executive Summary clarifying
  conclusions of, 111–112
Executive Summary requirements
  process, 116–117
review cycles, 125
writing outline using information from,
  90
yourself as member of, 83–84
pronouns, misused, 23–24
prose-based process explanation, 76–78
prototypes, 104

R

rapport, project team, 84–85
recommendations, Executive Summary,
  93, 112–114, 120
rectangle symbol, data flow diagrams, 39
reference material
creating body of document using, 104
as potential section of Executive
  Summary, 119
report specifications, 109, 137
requirements
adding diagram and section
  introductions, 74
business rules/non-functional, 72
data, 71

diagramming using prose-based
  structure, 78
diagramming using tabular structure,
  74–75
integrating diagram and, 78–80
language in, 69–70
numbering system, 70–71
statements, 69
requirements analysts, 17
requirements documents
capturing critical information. *See*
  information, capturing critical
  system
defining user interface design, 102
overview of, 2–3
qualities and purposes of, 5–6
reasons for writing, 3
relating story elements to, 4–5
software, 5–6
software vs. business, 6–7
templates. *See* templates, software
  requirements documents
why projects collapse without detailed,
  7–9
why we have failed to write, 9–12
requirements gathering process, Executive
  Summary, 116–117, 122
requirements summaries
adding to final document, 105–107
functional specification using, 127
generic outlines for, 92
managing requirements using, 128–129
robust outlines for, 94
software requirements documents and,
  136
using bookmarks for, 101
resources, excluding from Executive
  Summary, 112
responsibilities section, Executive
  Summary, 119
results of process, 63, 73
review cycles, 125
risks section, Executive Summary, 117,
  119
robust outlines, 93–94
roles section, Executive Summary, 119
rough diagrams. *See* draft diagrams